Martin Harris's Kirtland

EDITED BY RONALD E. ROMIG

John Whitmer Books
INDEPENDENCE, MISSOURI
2007

For Martin

Martin Harris's Kirtland
Edited by Ronald E. Romig

Published by
John Whitmer Books
Independence, Missouri
JohnWhitmerBooks.com

ISBN 978-1-934901-04-5
Printed in the United States of America

Copyrighted © 2007 by Ronald E. Romig
18 Oak Hill Cluster
Independence, MO 64057
rromig1@comcast.net

Without limiting the rights under copyright reserved above, no part of this publication may be reproduced, stored in or introduced into a retrieval system, or transmitted, in any form or by any means (electronic, mechanical, photocopying, recording or otherwise), without the prior written permission of the publisher.

Images, unless otherwise cited, are the copyrighted intellectual property of and provided courtesy of Community of Christ Libary-Archives, 1001 W. Walnut, Independence, MO 64050-3562.

Copyedited by Lavina Fielding Anderson
Artwork contributed by Anne Romig
Cover, interior design and maps by John C. Hamer
Typesetting by Ronald E. Romig

FRONT COVER IMAGE: Kirtland Temple, Henry Howe, 1846

BACK COVER IMAGE: Panorama of Kirtland, J. H. Kennedy, *Early Days of Mormonism* (N.Y.: Charles Scribner's Sons, 1888).

Table *of* Contents

Brief Biography of Martin Harris 5
Images of Martin Harris 19
Harris's Kirtland 20
John Clark, 1827 21
Organization of the Church 23
To Ohio 24
Arrival at Kirtland, March 1831 25
Sale of Palmyra Property, 1831; Journey to Missouri, June 1831 26
Consecration, August 1831 28
Harris's Predictions, 1832 29
A House of the Lord, 1832 30
Overseers of the Poor Warning, 1833; High Council, 1834 33
Visit to New York, 1835; House of the Lord, 1836 34
Description of Kirtland, 1836 36
Martin's Home Life 37
William West, 1837 38
Kirtland after the Exodus of the Saints 41
John Smith, 1838 42
William E. McLellin 43
Incorporation of the Church of Christ, 1838 44
George A. Smith, 1838 45
Stephen Burnett, 1838; Heber C. Kimball, 1839 46
Return to LDS Fellowship, 1838 47
Almon Babbitt, 1840 48
Mistaken Obituary, 1841; Rebaptism, 1842 49
Martin and the Shakers, 1844 50
Death of Joseph Smith, 1844 52
Sidney Rigdon, 1845 53
James J. Strang, 1846 54
Mission to England, 1846 55
William E. McLellin, 1847 57
James Brewster 61
James Bay, 1850; Reuben P. Harmon 62

Francis Gladden Bishop, 1851 ... 63
Ruben W. Alderman, 1852 ... 64
Ruben McBride, 1852 ... 65
David Dille, 1853 ... 67
Thomas Coburn, 1855 ... 68
Martin Harris's Proclamation, 1855 ... 70
Stephen Post, 1855, 1856 ... 72
Alone Again; William Smith ... 73
Joel Tiffany, 1859 ... 74
Francis M. Lyman, 1860 ... 76
William W. Blair, 1860 ... 77
Blair Interview, 1860 ... 81
David H. Cannon, 1861 ... 82
James McKnight, 1862; Stephen Post, 1864 ... 83
Joseph Smith III, 1866 ... 84
Christopher G. Crary; George Morse ... 85
Stephen Hart ... 86
Samuel F. Whitney ... 87
William H. Homer, 1869 ... 88
Edward Stevenson, February 1870 ... 92
Edward Stevenson, August 1870 ... 93
Journey to Utah ... 94
Martin's Absence ... 96
Harris Letter, November 1870 ... 98
Simon Smith, 1875 ... 99
Death of Martin Harris, William Homer, 1875 ... 100
Harris Obituary, 1875 ... 102
Funeral ... 105
"Interview with Martin Harris," Poem by William Pilkington ... 106
Additional Reading ... 108

Martin Harris's Kirtland

Martin Harris

A Brief Biography *of* Martin Harris

MARTIN HARRIS, the man who would sacrifice domestic peace, fortune and reputation to help establish the Mormon movement, was born 18 May 1783 in Easttown (Saratoga), Washington County, New York. Martin was the son of Nathan and Rhoda (Lapham) Harris. Martin moved with his father's family in his ninth year to the town of Palmyra, Ontario County (now Wayne), New York.* Eventually, the Harrises became one of the oldest and most comfortably situated pioneer families in the Palmyra area.

---

* Richard L. Anderson, *Investigating the Book of Mormon Witnesses* (Salt Lake City, Utah: Deseret Book Company, 1981), 111, hereinafter cited *IBMW*.

AS MARTIN MATURED, he married Lucy Harris, a first cousin, on 27 March 1808. The couple had six children. As a young man, Harris achieved considerable success. Besides farming, Martin engaged in civic and business affairs in the community. A former resident of Palmyra remembered Harris as "an industrious, hard-working farmer, shrewd in his business calculations, frugal in his habits, and... a prosperous man in the world."*

The couple's early married life was interrupted during Martin's service during the War of 1812. Martin started out as a teamster in the Battle of Buffalo and rose to the rank of first sergeant in the Thirty-ninth New York Militia, during the battle of Pultneyville in May 1814. He was honorably discharged. He inherited 150 acres of land from his father in Palmyra, New York. Within a few years his land holdings totaled 320 acres. Lucy Harris described him as industrious, attentive to domestic concerns, and an excellent provider and father. He was repeatedly elected as a local district overseer of highways. Martin's farming and sheep raising prowess is attested to by his recognition by the Ontario Agricultural Society for production of linen, cotton and woolen fabrics.†3 He also was a supporter of the Erie Canal project being constructed near his farm.

Harris stood about five feet, eight inches tall and was light of complexion with brown hair and blue eyes. During much of his life, Martin sported a Greek-style beard which he wore off the edge of his chin. In dressing for public appearances, Harris is said to have favored a gray suit topped off with a large stiff hat.

---

* James H. Reeves, statement, Palmyra Courier, 24 May 1872, cited in Anderson, *IBMW*, 96-97.

† Anderson, *IBMW*, 99; see also Susan Easton Black and Larry Porter, "For the Sum of Three Thousand Dollars," *Journal of Book of Mormon Studies* 14:2 (2005):6.

When young, Martin remained largely aloof from religious organizations. Harris became acquainted with the Joseph Smith Sr. family after their arrival in Palmyra in 1817. Becoming an intimate of the Smiths and their son Joseph Jr., Harris was present during the founding events of Mormonism. Harris was naturally curious when Joseph Smith mentioned visits from angelic beings. Martin's interest was piqued when Smith claimed to have recovered ancient American artifacts from a neighboring hill. Principal among these was a book of hieroglyphics said to be inscribed on plates having the appearance of gold. Harris asked Joseph for and received to his satisfaction a witness from the hand of God of the reality of these plates (D&C 5). Smith later credited Martin with helping preserve these artifacts.

Harris financially assisted Joseph and his wife Emma while relocating from the Palmyra area to Harmony, Pennsylvania. During their stay in Harmony, a significant portion of the story since known as the Book of Mormon was compiled. Harris assisted in this process by writing out words and sentences as Smith dictated. Martin Harris was around forty-five years old at this time, a well-to-do farmer and respected member of the Palmyra, New York, society. In February 1828 Joseph Smith asked Martin to further underwrite the publication of this religious narrative. Joseph provided Martin with a facsimile of characters said to be copied from the plates. While deciding whether to invest in this venture, Harris showed the transcription to scholars in Utica, Albany, and New York City. His experiences during this trip buttressed Martin's support for Smith's project.

Martin was Joseph Smith's primary scribe from 12 April through 14 June 1828. By this point, Smith's manuscript had reached a length of over 116 pages of hand-written material. Wishing to share this accomplishment

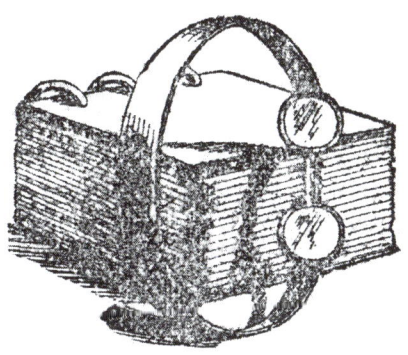

SPECTACLES AND PLATES

Book of Mormon Plates

with his wife and friends, Harris persuaded Joseph Smith to allow him to take the document to Palmyra. The manuscript pages disappeared while Martin served jury duty and attended to business. It has been reported that Lucy Harris feared Martin's involvement would lead to their financial ruin; so one night while her husband slept, she burned the pages in their stove. After this loss, the project halted for a time. Smith started again but no longer used Martin as a scribe. Another young acquaintance of Smith named Oliver Cowdery took on this role. Cowdery and Smith continued writing at a new location, the home of Peter Whitmer, Sr. in Fayette, Seneca County, New York.

In June 1829, Joseph Smith selected three witnesses for the purpose of affirming his religious and antiquarian claims. Martin was invited to serve as one of these primary witnesses, along with Oliver Cowdery and Peter Whitmer's son David. Harris was twenty years Oliver's and David's senior. The testimony of these witnesses has appeared in every edition of the Book of Mormon. This momentous activity impacted Harris's standing in the community, causing him to

An Angel instructs Joseph Smith and Martin Harris

become the target of rebuffs and rough comments from former associates.*

By the fall of 1829, a manuscript narrative had been readied for publication. Not having cash to underwrite the project, Martin pledged his farm, guaranteeing that the Egbert B. Grandin printing office in Palmyra would receive a full $3,000 payment for printing the Book of Mormon. All involved believed Martin would have no difficulty paying off the mortgage, expecting a

---

* James H. Reeves, statement, *Palmyra Courier*, 24 May 1872, cited in Anderson, *IBMW*, 96.

Baptism

demand for the book. Notice of the completion of publication appeared in the 26 March 1830 *Wayne Sentinel*, indicating that the Book of Mormon was available for purchase at Grandin's bookstore. However, recovery of the costs of publication proved difficult.

Harris was present on 6 April 1830 when a small band of Smith's believers organized as a church. On that day Martin was baptized by fellow witness Oliver Cowdery. Over the next year more than 100 members followed Martin's example in uniting with the fledgling movement.

In 1831, Smith asked adherents to move to Ohio. During May 1831 Martin led a group of fifty members to Kirtland, Ohio. But Martin's wife Lucy and their children remained in Palmyra. Over the next five years, Martin made periodic visits to New York to attend to family and business matters. The mortgage on Harris's farm for the Book of Mormon came due 5 February 1831. Martin subsequently sold part of his farm to Thomas Lakey on 7 April 1831.*

In Kirtland, Ohio Martin was ordained to the church's ecclesiastical office of high priest by fellow member Lyman Wight on 3 June 1831. During the summer of 1831, Smith asked Harris to accompany other High Priests to Missouri to help designate a gathering place in the West for disciples. During this trip, the frontier city of Independence, Jackson County, Missouri, was designated as the center place for building up a western colony. Smith called Missouri the land of Zion, anticipating the prompt inauguration of Christ's kingdom thereon.

---

* Martin Harris to Thomas Lakey, Wayne County New York Deeds, 7 April 1831, Book 10, 515–16, cited in Black and Porter, "For the Sum of Three Thousand Dollars," 11.

Independence, Missouri Public Square, 1831, by Henry K. Inouye, Jr.

Harris was asked to provide funds to purchase land in Jackson County, Missouri, to provide a place for a temple. In 1832, Harris was also inducted into a group of leaders tasked with financing and supervising the publication of a church periodical and book of scripture.

Martin undertook a missionary trip for the church to New York and Pennsylvania with his brother Emer Harris. Together they baptized more than one hundred converts.

On 17 February 1834, Harris's standing was further elevated when he was selected as a member of the Kirtland High Council. In May 1834 he volunteered to accompany Zion's Camp to Missouri. The expeditionary force hoped to restore members who had been forcibly displaced from their lands in Jackson County the previous year.

On 14 February 1835, the three witnesses to the Book of Mormon were accorded the privilege of selecting the church's first Quorum of Twelve Apostles.*

Though Martin advanced no further in the leadership of the church, he participated in the dedication of the Kirtland Temple in March 1836. Later that year, Martin's wife, Lucy, died in Palmyra, New York and he married Caroline Young, a niece of Brigham Young, 1 November 1836. Caroline was about thirty years Martin's junior. During their life together they had seven children.

---

* D&C 16: 6a (CoC); 18:37-38 (LDS).

Joseph Smith depended on older men for the expertise and satability necessary to successfully advance his religious aims. However, as the church developed, Martin felt he was being overlooked for positions of high standing. This may relate to a perception in and outside the church that Harris had a loose tongue and was prone to excessive religious enthusiasm. Ohio church member Ezra Booth, who accompanied Harris to Missouri in 1831, wrote: "Martin Harris is what may be called a great talker, an extravagant boaster; so much so, that he renders himself disagreeable to many of this society."*

As a young man, Harris embraced the Jeffersonian-Jacksonian monetary idea favoring gold and silver—while rejecting the use of paper currency. As a result, in 1837 he refused to support the church-initiated Kirtland Safety Society Anti-Banking Co. Thereby, Martin avoided the uncountable loss suffered by many who participated in the speculative venture. But Harris's actions reinforced a perception he was unsupportive of church leaders. Martin himself also gradually lost confidence in Joseph Smith's leadership. This course resulted in Harris's release from the high council on 3 September 1837. Complications from this fractured relationship led to his excommunication from the church during the last week of December 1837. Having been the target of rebuffs before in Palmyra, Martin deeply resented such treatment from former friends.

With the disintegration of the Kirtland-based economy, the Church abandoned Ohio, moving its headquarters to Far West, Mis-

A portion of a Kirtland Safety Society Anti-Banking Co. note

---

* Ezra Booth to Rev. Ira Eddy, 2 October 1831, Ohio Star 2 (20 October 1831): 3. Citizens of the Palmyra, New York area described Harris as a good business man, "but on moral and religious subjects, he was perfectly visionary—sometimes advocating one sentiment, and sometimes another." Statement by fifty-one citizens of Palmyra, New York, 4 December 1833, Eber D. Howe, *Mormonism Unvailed* (Painesville, Ohio), 261.

Ann Lee, Mother Shaker

souri, in 1838. Harris remained behind. In November 1838, Martin purchased a hundred-acre farm in Kirtland about one mile southeast of the Temple.* Kirtland was Harris's primary residence for the next thirty years. As a result, Martin had no part in the movement's sad experiences attending the Missouri Mormon War and the fall of Nauvoo.

In successive years, the solitary witness's religious yearnings were never fully satisfied. Though adrift from his former spiritual moorings, Harris avoided the human tendency to seek retaliation. Martin remaining faithful to his witness "that the Mormon cause was founded on objective truth as he had experienced it" in 1829.†

Following the Kirtland exodus, other former acolytes like Harris cast off Smith and occupied the Temple. This party rallied around former Smith aide Warren Parrish and attempted to reorganize the church as they believed it to have formerly existed. In accordance with Ohio law, corporate officers "were chosen and the original church name was incorporated, with Joseph Coe, Martin Harris, and Cyrus Smalling named as trustees of the 'Church of Christ.'"‡

Harris subsequently withdrew from Parish's group when fellow adherents renounced the Book of Mormon. By July 1838, Harris was fellowshipping again in Kirtland with others supporting Smith's leadership.

Harris was rebaptized by 18 July 1840. He asked for rebaptism again when Lyman Wight, one of the Church's Twelve Apostles from Nauvoo, passed through

---

* Judge Stevens Deed, 15 November 1838, Lake County (Ohio) Historical Society. Harris paid $800 for a hundred and five acre farm on Lot number 45 near Kirtland.

† Anderson, *IBMW*, 111.
‡ H. Michael Marquardt, "Martin Harris: The Kirtland Years, 1831-1870," *Dialogue*, 35, no. 3 (Fall 2002): 13.

Kirtland in 1842. But Martin's reformations were short lived.

In 1843, reports of powerful spiritual manifestations occurring in nearby Shaker communities produced a lot of excitement throughout Ohio. Martin was attracted for a time by the teachings of Mother Ann Lee, founder of the Shaker movement.

The emergence of several potential leaders of the Restoration movement after Joseph Smith's death in 1844 rekindled Martin's interest in Mormonism. "Harris, like many church members, did not know whom to follow and changed his loyalty several times, choosing first one supposed successor, then another."*

Joseph Smith's brother, William B. Smith, representing one of these claimants, James J. Strang, came to Kirtland in 1846. James Strang also turned out for the event. Strang and Smith conducted a conference in the Kirtland Temple and organized a stake of the church. Harris was among those attracted by Strang's declaration of authority and was selected as a member of the organization's Kirtland Stake High Council.†

William B. Smith

Harris also agreed to serve a mission to England. Lester Brooks, another James Strang representative, accompanied Harris to Great Britain. Harris's poor reception in England cut the trip short and Martin soon returned to Kirtland. Martin as well as many others from the Kirtland area soon rejected Strang's claims. In the aftermath of this local excitement, Harris returned to his farm and cared for the Temple. Martin also continued occasional visits to Palmyra, New York, where some of his children still lived and he held land.‡

---

* Ibid., 19.
† *Voree Herald* 1, no. 9 (September, 1846):1.
‡ Anderson, *IBMW*, 113.

Lyman O. Littlefield

Former apostle William E. McLellin next appeared in Kirtland and began advocating for David Whitmer as Joseph Smith's legitimate successor. McLellin based his claims on Smith's ordination of Whitmer as president of the church in Missouri, in 1834. Martin Harris affiliated with "McLellin's Church of Christ by baptism, confirmation, and reordination 'to the same authority... held in the Church before.'"*

McLellin's movement quickly ran its course, leaving Martin unaffiliated again. By this time Martin was sixty-six. In 1849, Harris made another journey in New York to testify of the truth of the Book of Mormon. A Rochester editor reported that, while he was there, Harris supported his witness "with the fluency and zeal of a devotee."†

By 1851 Martin was back in Kirtland, where the prophet Francis Gladden Bishop preached in the Kirtland Temple to proclaim yet another version of Mormonism. Harris aligned himself with Bishop for a time but was soon adrift again. During this period, it appears that Martin no longer operated his farm but supported himself by working for neighbors.‡

Around 1855, Martin told Mormon visitor Thomas Colburn that he had found "no satisfaction; [but] had concluded he would wait until the Saints returned to Jackson Co., and then he would repair there." Colburn encouraged Harris to gather to Utah. And before Colburn left, Martin concluded "that he should go there as soon as he could get away."§

---

* "Things in Kirtland," The Ensign of Liberty 1, no. 4 (January 1848):56; quoted in Marquardt, 26.

† *Rochester Daily American* (16 November 1849); cited by Anderson, *IBMW*, 113.
‡ Stephen H. Hart, statement, November 1884, *Naked Truths about Mormonism* 1 (April 1888):3.
§ Thomas Colburn to Elder Snow, 2 May 1855, *St. Louis Luminary* 1 (5 May 1855):95; quoted in Marquardt, "Martin Harris," 31.

But, Martin got caught up again in local religious excitement, when a Miss Sexton, a spirit medium from Cleveland, Ohio, voiced a revelation purportedly from Moses, Elias, Elijah, and John. In May 1855, Martin published this proclamation in the form of an eight-page pamphlet, titled "A Proclamation and a Warning Voice Unto All People"* Harris circulated the pamphlet throughout the neighborhood and even forwarded a copy to Brigham Young.†

In October 1855, Stephen Post came to Kirtland and allied with William B. Smith in another attempt to reorganize the church. Harris assisted Post and William Smith to convene yet another conference in the Kirtland Temple.

In 1856, the Harris family was again urged to gather to Utah. Martin's wife Caroline (Young) was the sister of Louisa (Young) Littlefield. The Lyman Littlefield family, living in western Iowa, was ready to proceed on to Utah. Louisa urged Martin and his family to join their party. Martin was seventy-two and

Martin Harris, Jr.

Caroline thirty-nine. And at this time their children were: Martin, Jr. (28 January 1838), Caroline (circa 1839, died by 1850 census), Julia (29 April 1842), John (11 July 1845), Sarah (circa 1849, died by 1860 census), Solomon (1 December 1854), all born in Kirtland.‡ Also, Caroline was pregnant again, expecting their seventh child.

In the end, Caroline and the children went west, while Martin remained in Kirtland. A daughter, Ida May Harris, was born on 27 May 1856, in Iowa. Caroline and the children appear in the 1856 Rockford Township, Pottawattamie County, Iowa census. Caroline and the children

---

* Stephen Post, journal, 5 October 1885, LDS Church Archives, cited in Marquardt, "Martin Harris," 32.
† Martin Harris to Brigham Young, 13 August 1885, Brigham Young Collection, LDS Church Archives.
‡ Marquardt, "Martin Harris," 14-15.

completed passage to Utah with Lyman Littlefield's family.

Harris was living in Kirtland in 1857, still associated with William Smith's movement. But by 1858, Harris and William Smith parted ways. "Harris drove Wm. Smith out of the place."*

In January 1859, Joel Tiffany, editor of *Tiffany's Monthly*, a Spiritualist publication, visited Kirtland and interviewed Martin. This interview gave Martin a grand opportunity to reaffirm his witness of early experiences with Joseph Smith and the founding events of Mormonism.†

Martin Harris's activities are further disclosed in the 1860 census records with Harris enumerated as a part of the George Harris household in Kirtland Township. George Harris was Martin's son with Lucy. Harris described himself to the 1860 census taker as a "Mormon preacher." Rent from Martin's farm was his main support. Martin was now religiously affiliated with former LDS members Zadock Brooks and Leonard Rich. Visiting Reorganized Church Apostle William W. Blair reported, that they "have formed

William Harrison Homer

an organization of 7 Souls[,] 4 of them are women[.]" The Brooks group used the Temple regularly for worship. This afforded Harris the opportunity to continue in the role of Temple caretaker and guide.‡ Francis M. Lyman, an LDS missionary on his way to England, was one of the many visitors Harris showed through the Temple during this time.§

James McKnight visited Martin in February 1862 and reported that Harris was basically homeless, his son George, "a worthless scape-grace, with whom he lived, being in prison and the house deserted. Yet... he has never failed

---

* Enoch Beese, quoted in Wilford Woodruff Journal, 22 June 1858, 5:198-99; cited in Marquardt, "Martin Harris," 35.
† "Mormonism—II," Tiffany's Monthly 5 (August 1859):163-70, quoted ibid., 35.

‡ Apostle William W. Blair, of the Reorganized Church visited the Temple on 9 August 1860, "Memoirs-No. III," Saints' Herald 37 (12 July 1890):460-61; both quoted ibid., 36-37.
§ Francis M. Lyman, June 1860, "My Mission," *The Contributor* 17 (April 1896):352.

Orson Pratt

to confirm his testimony of the truth of that Book."*

For the next five years or so, Martin was penniless. George Morse, a small boy at the time, recalled, Martin Harris... was in destitute circumstances and used to visit around among the people, stopping several days at a time among different families."† Kirtland township trustee Christopher G. Crary said, "Complaint was made to me that Martin Harris was destitute of a home, poorly clothed, feeble, burdensome to friends, and that he ought to be taken to the poor-house." A family living in the Harris house agreed to care for him, thus preventing Harris's installation in the county poor-house.‡

Martin's older brother Preserved had also remained in the Kirtland area after the Mormon exodus. But Preserved died on 18 April 1867 at Mentor, Lake County, Ohio.§

Beginning in 1869, William H. Homer, Edward Stevenson, and other LDS members extended help to Martin that enabled him gather to Utah. Edward Stevenson accompanied Martin, who was still quite vigorous at age eighty-seven, on the train to Utah. Along the way, Stevenson arranged for an interview with the *Iowa State Register* in Des Moines, Iowa. The editor reported, "The old gentleman evidently loves to relate the incidents with which he was personally connected, and he does it with wonderful enthusiasm."¶

The pair arrived in Salt Lake City, Utah, on 30 August 1870. There Martin was invited to publicly testify about his experience as a Book of Mormon witness.

---

* 24. James McKnight to George Q. Cannon, 27 February 1862, *Millennial Star* 24 (19 April 1862):251, quoted ibid., 38.
† George Morse, Willoughby Republican, 29 June 1921, quoted ibid., 38.
‡ Christopher G. Crary, Pioneer and Personal Reminiscences (Marshalltown, Iowa: 1893), 44-45.
§ RootsWeb.com; http://worldconnect.rootsweb.com/cgi-bin/igm.cgi?op=GET&db=buchroeder&id=I567210042
¶ Daily Iowa State Register, 28 August 1870, cited in Anderson, IBMW, 114.

Nancy (Homer) Harris, wife of Martin Harris Jr., in whose home the aged witness spent his declining years.

Martin was rebaptized in the Endowment House by Stevenson and confirmed by Orson Pratt, John Taylor, Wilford Woodruff, and Joseph F. Smith.*

In Utah, Martin was reunited with his sister, Mrs. Naomi Bent, and visited Caroline, now married and sealed to John Catley Davis, and his children. It was his first time meeting Ida May, born en route to Utah. Martin's eldest daughter Julia and his brother Emer Harris died the year before Martin arrived.

Harris went to live with Martin Harris, Jr. his oldest son by Caroline, and daughter-in-law Nancy (Homer) Harris in Smithfield. Soon after, the family moved across the valley to Clarkston. "This Clarkston home soon became a center with a beaten path leading to its door, a constant stream of visitors from far and near coming to pay their respects to Martin Harris."†

At the age of ninety-two, Martin Harris died on 10 July 1875, in Clarkston, Cache County, Utah. His grave is distinguished by a granite pillar designating him as one of the Three Witnesses of the Book of Mormon. Over the course of his life, his personal witness, always given with conviction, positively impacted the lives of scores of people.‡

—*Brief Biography* drawn from: Rhett Stephens James, "Harris, Martin," *Encyclopedia of Mormonism* 4 vols. (New York: Macmillan Publishing, 1992), 2: 574-76; and H. Michael Marquardt, "Martin Harris: The Kirtland Years, 1831-1870," *Dialogue: A Journal of Mormon Thought* 35, no. 3 (Fall 2002):1-40; Christin Craft Mackay and Lachlan Mackay, "A Time of Transition: The Kirtland Temple, 1838-1800," *John Whitmer Historical Association Journal* 18 (1998):133-48.

---

* Journal History of the LDS Church, 17 September 1870.

† William H. Homer Jr., "'Publish It upon the Mountains:' The Story of Martin Harris," The Improvement Era 55, no. 7 (July 1955):507.

‡ Anderson, IBMW, 114.

Images *of* Martin Harris

Four views of Martin Harris, top and bottom right courtesy LDS Church Archives.

Martin Harris's Kirtland

NO INDIVIDUAL is more representative of the broad range of Mormonism's religious experience as lived out at Kirtland, Ohio, than Martin Harris. This book reproduces many documents detailing Harris's life and experiences. Such historical sources shed light about Martin's continuing involvement with the Mormon Movement and his activities after most Mormons left Kirtland in 1838. And finally, this work will explore the close connection between Martin's story and the history of the Kirtland Temple after the exodus.

John Clark, 1827

THE STORY OF Mormonism and how Martin Harris came to be part of it begins with an assertion. On 22 September 1827 a young man by the name of Joseph Smith Jr. of the state of New York, unearthed a religious history of the ancient inhabitants of the Americas. In a short time, Martin Harris becomes associated with Smith in this religious narrative.

As a former resident and minister of Palmyra, New York, area in 1827, Reverend John A. Clark was a life-long observer of Mormonism. Clark prepared the following account focusing on his encounter with Martin Harris during the earliest days of Mormonism:

It was early in the autumn of 1827 that Martin Harris called at my house in Palmyra, one morning about sunrise. His whole appearance indicated more than unusual excitement, and he had scarcely passed the threshold of my dwelling, before he inquired whether he could see me alone, remarking, that he had a matter to communicate that he wished to be strictly confidential. Previous to this, I had but very slight acquaintance with Mr. Harris. He had occasionally attended divine service in our church. I had heard him spoken of as a farmer in comfortable circumstances, residing in the country a short distance from the village, and distinguished by certain peculiarities in his character. He had been, if I mistake not, at one period a member of the Methodist Church, and subsequently had identified himself with the Universalists. At this time, however in his religious views, he seemed to be floating upon the sea of uncertainty.

He had evidently quite an extensive knowledge of the Scriptures, and possessed a manifest disputatious turn of mind. As I subsequently learned, Mr. Harris had always been a firm believer in dreams, and visions, and supernatural appearances, such as apparitions and ghosts, and therefore was a fit subject for such men as Smith and his colleagues to operate upon. On the occasion just referred to, I invited him to accompany me to my study.... He said he verily believed that an important epoch had arrived—that a great flood of light was about to burst upon the world, and that the scene of divine manifesta-

Book of Mormon Characters

tion was to be immediately around us. In explanation of what he meant he then proceeded to remark that a Golden Bible had recently been dug from the earth, where it had been deposited for thousands of years, and that this would be found to contain such disclosures as would settle all religious controversies, and speedily bring on the glorious millennium. That this mysterious book, which no human eye of the present generation had yet seen, was in the possession of Joseph Smith, jr., ordinarily known in the neighborhood under the more familiar designation of Joe Smith; that there had been a revelation made to him by which he had discovered this sacred deposit, and two transparent stones through which, as a sort of spectacles, he could read the bible, although the box or ark that contained it, had not been opened; and that by looking through those mysterious stones, he had transcribed from one of the leaves of this book, the characters.... He went on to relate the particulars in regard to the discovery and possession of this marvelous book....

— John A. Clark, "The Mormons," *Warsaw Signal*, 2, no. 10 (14 July 1841): 1.

WITH THE HELP of Martin Harris, Oliver Cowdery, David Whitmer, and others, Joseph Smith produced a translation into the English language of this history known as the Book of Mormon.

Organization of the Church, 6 April 1830

Following the publication of the Book of Mormon, Smith organized the "Church of Christ," on 6 April 1830.

To Ohio

WITHIN A YEAR OF the publication of the Book of Mormon the church was astir, establishing a colony in Missouri and locating its headquarters to Kirtland, Ohio. About one thousand converts were drawn into the church within a short period of time. On 22 February 1831, Joseph Smith wrote to Harris from Kirtland, Ohio requesting him to "bring or cause to be brought all the books [of Mormon in his possession] to Kirtland."10 About 9 March 1831, Harris left Palmyra for Kirtland. *The Wayne* (Palmyra) *Sentinel* newspaper places Harris's departure in May 1831 from Palmyra for the promised land of Ohio:

SEVERAL families, numbering about fifty souls, took up their line of march from this town [Palmyra] last week for the "promised land," among who was Martin Harris, one of the original believers in the "Book of Mormon." Mr. Harris was among the early settlers of this town, and has ever borne the character of an honorable and upright man, and an obliging and benevolent neighbor. He had secured to himself by honest industry a respectable fortune—and has left a large circle of acquaintants and friends to pity his delusion.

—*Wayne Sentinel* 8 (27 May 1831):3.

Many members traveled to Ohio by steamboat.

Martin Harris's Arrival at Kirtland

MARTIN HARRIS WAS forty-seven when he arrived at Painesville, Ohio, on Saturday, 12 March, 1831, bringing with him a large supply of Books of Mormon. Harris's eccentric personality was immediately noted by the local paper:

HE IMMEDIATELY planted himself in the bar-room of the hotel.... He told all about the gold plates. Angels, Spirits, and Jo Smith.—He had seen and handled them all, by the power of God!... He was very flippant, talking fast and loud, in order that others could not interpose an opinion counter to him. Every idea that he advanced, he knew to be absolutely true, as he said, by the spirit and power of God... declaring, that all who believed the new Bible would see Christ within fifteen years, and all who did not would absolutely be destroyed and dam'd [damned].

—"Martin Harris," *The Telegraph* (Painesville, Ohio) 2, No. 39 (15 March 1831):3.

Martin's stories, by Anne Romig

Sale of Palmyra Property, 1831

SHORTLY AFTER THIS, Harris returned to Palmyra and sold 151 acres of his farm land to Thomas Lakey for $3,000. On 3 May 1831, Harris also signed over certain personal items into the hands of Thomas Lakey, including "300 Books of Mormon to be sold for $1.25 & account to the said Harris $1.00 for each copy."

—Deed, recorded in Deed Liber 10:515-16, Wayne County, Lyons, New York.

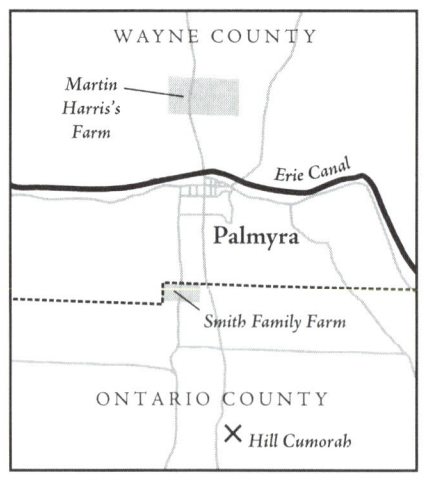

Palmyra, New York, Map courtesy of John Hamer.

Trip To Missouri, 1831

HARRIS RETURNED TO Ohio by early June 1831, in time to participate in one of the early church's most daring adventures. Church leaders in Ohio had received encouraging news from five missionaries, who had been dispatched the previous year to take the story of the Book of Mormon to Native Americans beyond Missouri in the great American West. The Lamanite missionaries' accomplishment prompted a second great missionary journey. In preparation for this mission, on 3 June 1831, the Church of Christ at Kirtland ordained twenty-three key leaders to the high priesthood. Martin Harris was one of them. During a four-day conference, Joseph Smith designated fourteen teams of missionaries to travel to Missouri during the summer of 1831. Martin was especially selected to accompany key leaders during this journey of exploration to Missouri. Joseph Smith's history chronicles their departure.

ON THE 19TH OF June, in company with Sidney Rigdon, Martin Harris, Edward Partridge, William W. Phelps, Joseph Coe, Algernon S. Gilbert and his wife, I started from Kirtland, Ohio, for the land of Missouri, agreeable to the commandment before received, wherein it was promised that if we were faithful, the land of our inheritance, even the place for the city of the New Jerusalem, should be revealed. We went by wagon, canal boats, and stages to Cincinnati.... We left Cincinnati in a steamer, and landed at Louisville, Kentucky, where we were detained three days in waiting for a steamer to convey us to St. Louis. At St. Louis, myself, Brothers Harris, Phelps, Partridge and Coe, went by land on foot to Independence, Jackson county, Missouri, where we arrived about the middle of July, and the rest of the company came by water a few days later.

—*History of the LDS Church*, 1:188.

Harris's Journey to Missouri, Map courtesy of John Hamer.

Consecration

WHILE IN JACKSON County, Harris received a revelation counseling him to lay his monies before Bishop Edward Partridge as an example to encourage others to consecrate their resources to advance the colonization of Jackson County, Missouri.

AND NOW I GIVE unto you further directions concerning this land. It is wisdom in me that my servant Martin Harris should be an example unto the church, in laying his moneys before the bishop of the church. And also this is a law unto every man that cometh unto this land, to receive an inheritance; and he shall do with his moneys according as the law directs. And it is wisdom also, that there should be lands purchased in Independence, for the place of the storehouse: and also for the house of the printing.

And other directions, concerning my servant Martin Harris, shall be given him of the spirit, that he may receive his inheritance as seemeth him good. And let him repent of his sins, for he seeketh the praise of the world.

—D&C 58.

IN RESPONSE, HARRIS furnished money to purchase land for a temple. Martin was a participant during the 3 August 1831, dedication of the Temple Lot. After the ceremony, a party of ten left to return to the East. They started down the Missouri River traveling by canoe. Before long, Smith, Rigdon, and Cowdery withdrew and continued on by land, leaving Martin and others to return to Ohio on their own.

Independence, Missouri, Temple Lot Dedication, by Henry K. Inouye Jr.

Predictions, 1832

IN SEPTEMBER 1832, Harris, who was known for his prophetic predictions, wrote the following two statements for a friend, "who placed them upon the wall of his office":

> I DO HEREBY ASSERT and declare that in four years from the date hereof, every sectarian and religious denomination in the United States, shall be broken down, and every Christian shall be gathered unto the Mormonites, and the rest of the human race shall perish. If these things do not take place, I will hereby consent to have my hand separated from my body.
>
> MARTIN HARRIS.

> WITHIN FOUR years from September 1832, there will not be one wicked person left in the United States; that the righteous will be gathered to Zion [Missouri] and that there will be no President over these United States after that time.
>
> MARTIN HARRIS.

—E. D. Howe, *Mormonism Unvailed*, 14.

Martin Harris as a young man, by Anne Romig

A House *of the* Lord

WITHIN TWO YEARS of the move to Ohio, the church was instructed to build a house of worship to become known as the Kirtland Temple. Joseph Smith articulated this magnificent goal, convincing the body of believers to

...establish a house, even a house of prayer, a house of fasting, a house of faith, a house of learning, a house of glory, a house of order, a house of God.

—D&C 85:36b (CoC),
D&C 88:119 (LDS).

THEREIN ITS representatives hoped to be endowed with spiritual power as described in the New Testament on the Day of Pentecost. Joining in the common labors of the community of believers, Martin did all he could to help the church realize its glorious dream. Benjamin F. Johnson recalled:

A stone quarry at [an] easy distance was opened to obtain the rock for its construction. But such was the poverty of the people at the time of breaking ground for its foundation, that there was not a scraper and hardly a plow that could be obtained among the Saints.

—Benjamin F. Johnson,
My Life's Review
(Independence, Missouri:
Zion's Printing and
Publishing Co., 1947), 16.

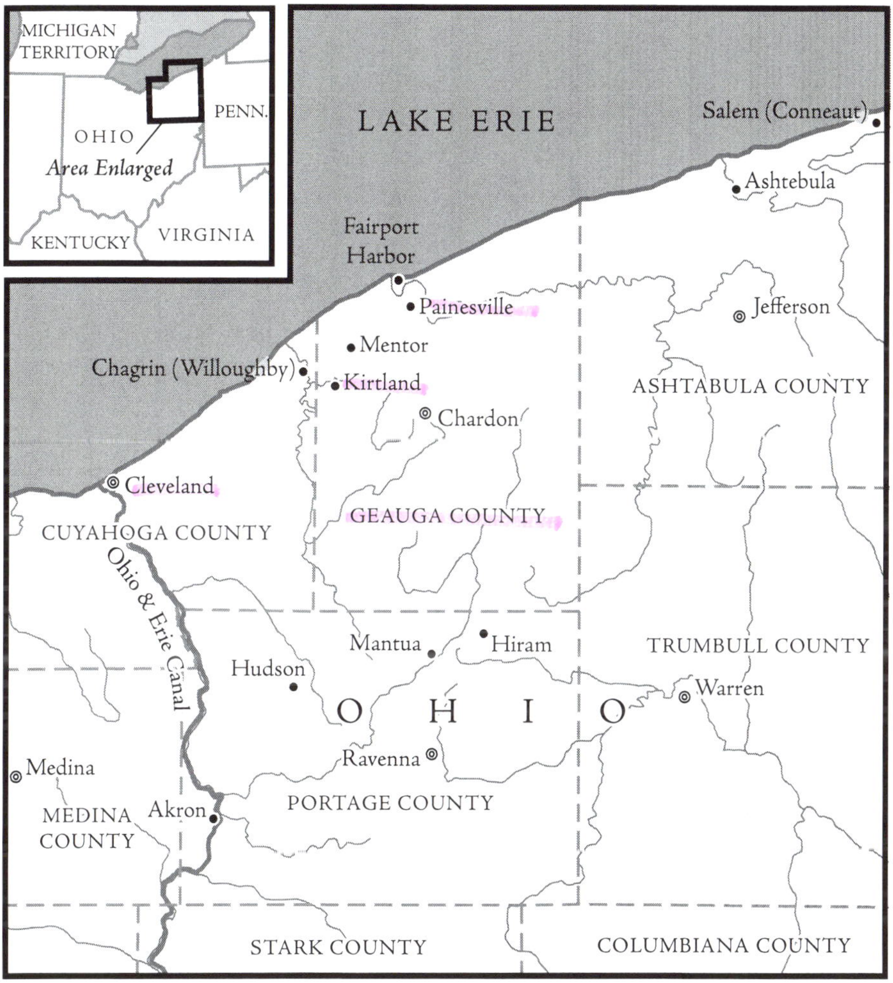

Western Reserve area of Ohio in the 1830s. Map courtesy of John Hamer.

MARTIN HARRIS'S KIRTLAND

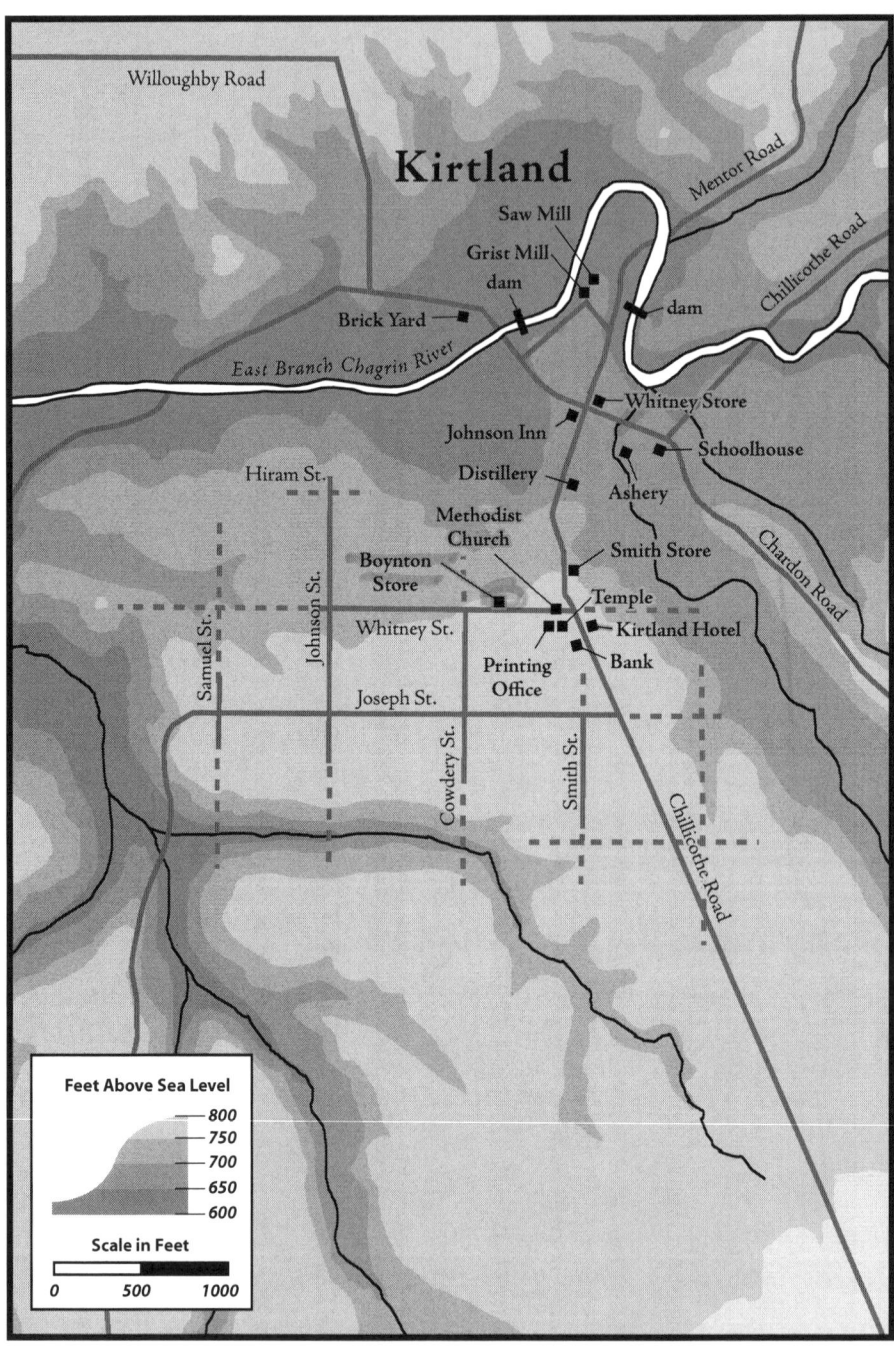

Kirtland in the 1830s. Map courtesy of John Hamer.

Warned by Overseers of the Poor, 1833

FROM THE NON-Mormon perspective, Martin Harris was unwelcome in Kirtland. Former citizens believed Harris would likely become dependent upon public support if they allowed him to remain in Kirtland Township. On 20 December 1833, Constable Steven Sherman served notice on behalf of the township Overseers of the Poor warning Martin Harris to depart the township immediately.

—Kirtland Township Records, Lake County Historical Society.

High Council, 1834

High Council, by Jack Garnier

THOUGH called before the Kirtland High Council on 12 February 1834 for spreading stories about Joseph Smith, [see *History of the LDS Church* 2:26], Martin was set apart as a member of the church's Standing High Council on 17 February 1834. This council helped settle important difficulties within the church.

JOSEPH SMITH, SR., John Smith, Joseph Coe, John Johnson, Martin Harris, John S. Carter, Jared Carter, Oliver Cowdery, Samuel H. Smith, Orson Hyde, Sylvester Smith, and Luke Johnson, high priests, were chosen to be a standing council for the church, by the unanimous voice of the council.... Oliver Cowdery, Orson Hyde, Clerks.

—D&C 99:2a (CoC), D&C 102:3 (LDS)

Visit to Palmyra, New York, 1835

IN-BETWEEN HIS various exploits, Councilor Harris managed periodic visits to his family in New York. In the fall of 1835, Bishop Edward Partridge stayed with Harris in Palmyra, New York.

THE 7 [1835] WENT to Palmyra... and lodged with Br. Martin Harris, we passed the hill Cumorah about 3 miles south of Palmyra It is a hill perhaps 100 feet high running from a trifle west of north to a little east of south, the north end breaks off very square, and when from a distance we view it the sides appear steep like the roof of a house....

—Edward Partridge, Journal, 1835-36, MS 4881, LDS Church Archives

House of the Lord, 1836

BY 1836, through the united labors of its members, the community finalized the construction of a remarkable structure designed for worship and learning. Church members experienced a season of enormous joy attending the dedication of the Kirtland Temple in March 1836.

WITHIN THE Kirtland Temple one may not only encounter the Spirit of God, but also a palpable presence of a dynamic spiritual heritage. The extended Restoration family views the Kirtland Temple as sacred. Such movement-wide kinship may be experienced in no other place more so than within this sacred building.

Kirtland Temple, constructed 1833-36.

1836 Description *of* Kirtland

The community of Kirtland, Ohio, seen from the northwest.

THE EDITORS OF THE church periodical, *The Messenger and Advocate* provided the following word sketch of Kirtland, as it appeared 1836:

A VERY considerable branch of the Chagrin river runs in a diagonal direction through the North part of this town, making... good mill sites.... There are two saw mills, one grist-mill, one fulling-mill, and one carding machine in the short distance of two miles. A steam saw-mill 35 by 60, designed for two saws is being erected in this place.... As you approach the place from the North you come to the brow of a hill.... Here the eye... catches the Lord's House on a beautiful eminence or table land on the south side of the stream, at an altitude of from 80 to 100 feet from its bed.... The house of the Lord is here, and a congregation of between 800 and 1000 assemble in it... every Lord's day.... We have one public inn or tavern, three stores of dry good kept by our brethren, and two by other people, making five in all, and quite a number of mechanics of different occupations.... Our village has been laid out in a regular plot, and calculated for streets to cross each other at right angles.

—"To the Saints Abroad," *The Messenger and Advocate*, 2, no. 10 (July 1836): 349.

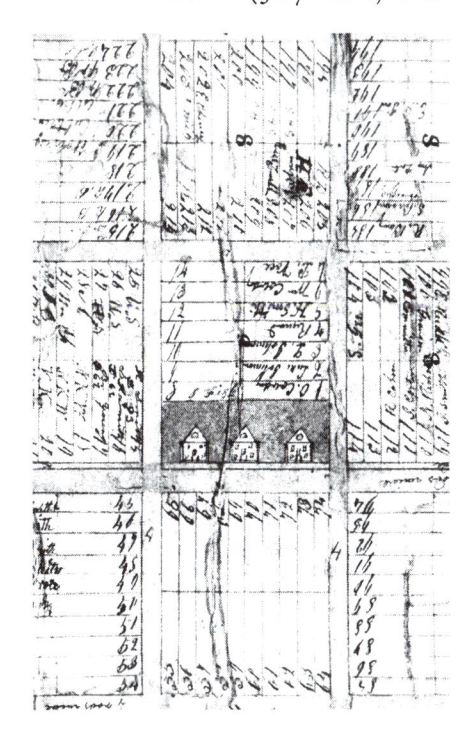

Plat of Kirtland, ca. 1834, original at LDS Church Archives.

Home Life

IN 1836, AFTER SEVERAL years of separation from his family, Martin's wife, Lucy, died at Palmyra, New York. The dynamic Kirtland community prompted a period of optimism and new beginnings. On 1 November 1836, Martin married Caroline Young. Caroline was Brigham Young's niece, the daughter of John and Theodocia (Kimball) Young. Having been born 17 May 1816 in Hector, Schuyler County, New York, Caroline was about thirty years Martin's junior. Martin's and Caroline's first child, Martin Harris Jr., was born at Kirtland in January 1838. During their life together they had seven children.

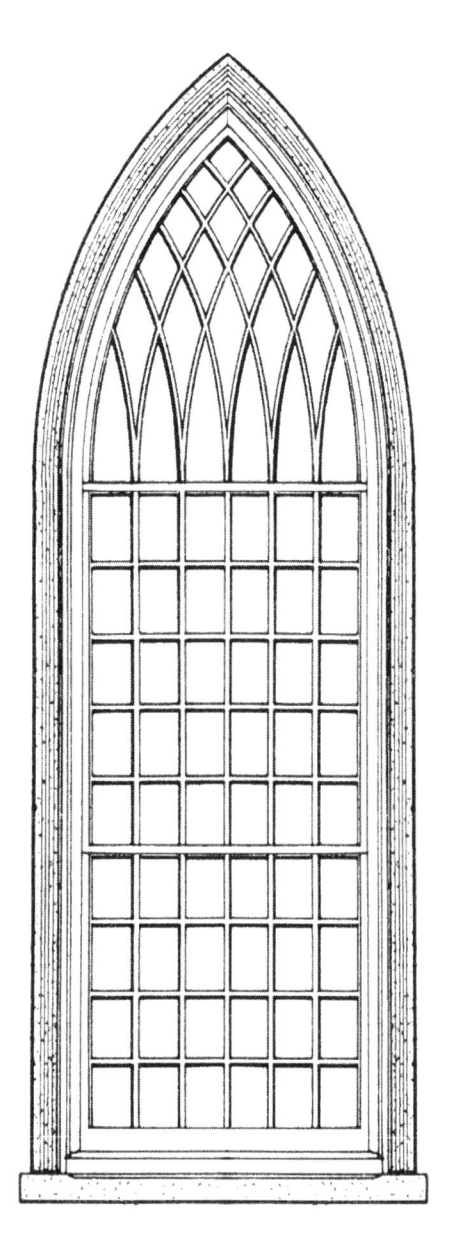

William West, 1837

WILLIAM WEST, A resident of northern Ohio, visited Kirtland in 1837 and left a detailed description of the Kirtland Temple. William S. West's identity remains obscure. According to his booklet, he was living in Braceville, Trumbull Co., Ohio. It is possible that West was a member of the Disciples' Church (the Campbellites).

THE AUTHOR OF THIS work having ascertained that people in general were very ignorant of the movements of the Mormons, determined as publishing to the world some of the most important facts in his possession; but not being contented with his present store of information, he immediately repaired to Kirtland, where he spend a few days in viewing their growing village, and magnificent temple, their Egyptian mummies and records, asking questions, &c.

... The lot on which the Temple is situated is in the best part of the village, and is forty rods long, and twelve wide. This lot is the personal property of Joseph Smith, Jr. For the truth of this see revelation given to Enoch, eighth paragraph, to be found in the Mormon Book of Doctrine and Covenants, page 243. And we learn from the sixth paragraph of said revelation, that other public buildings are to be erected on the same lot, all of which must of course be under Smith's control. The fact that the Mormons have been duped to give this valuable lot to their prophet Joseph Smith, and expend more than $30,000 in building a Temple on it is a positive proof that they are dupes indeed. This Temple is built of stone, and the outside is finished with a hard cement, it is 80 feet long, and sixty wide. It is lighted with

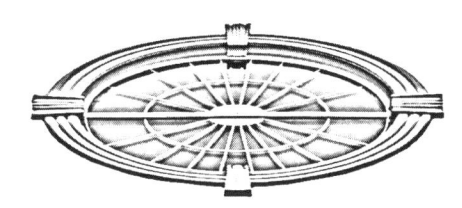

WINDOWS:

32 Gothic each	75 panes
3 Venetial each	118 panes
10 Dormer each	24 panes
2 Square gable each	20 panes
1 Circular	36 panes
2 half circle each	7 panes
Basement each	18 panes

Total multiplied and added=3156.

In front, at the height of 45 feet from the ground is this inscription, in gilt letters:

HOUSE OF THE LORD BUILT BY THE CHURCH OF THE LATTER DAY SAINTS, A. D. 1834.

I paid twenty-five cents for going through the Temple, and seeing the mummies and records, which excited my curiosity so much that I went the next day and examined them again. Upon entering the first story the keeper took off his hat, I did the same and asked him if that was the rule, he said it was. Indeed, the sublime appearance of that apartment, when the vails [sic] are unfurled, seem to enjoin sacred reverence. There is a pulpit in the west end for the Melchizedek priesthood, composed of four seats parallel with each other, those in the rear suitably elevated, and each seat calculated for three officers and accommodated with a suitable desk, which is ornamented with a cushion and fringe, and a curve for each occupant, on the front of which is the initials of his office, in gilt letters. The desk of the front seat consists of the leaves of the communion table, upon which are the initials of its occupants, in letters of stain. There is also a pulpit in the east end for the Aaronic priesthood, which is of the same construction.

The vails by which the house in divided into quarters, are of canvass, painted white, and are rolled up or drawn at pleasure, by means of cords which come down the pillars concealed, and are worked with cranks; also each official seat is completely vailed, both sides and front; these are also worked with cords which come in the seats concealed. The second story is not finished; but is to be of the same pattern, except the official seats which are not so much elevated. I have been particular in describing this apartment, because I have never seen any account of it before the world. For further accounts of the Temple see Mormon *Advocate* of July, 1835, also of Jun. 1837.

The Mormons have four mummies, and a quantity of records, written on papyrus, in Egyptian hieroglyphics, which were brought from the catacombs near Thebes, in Egypt. They say that the mummies were Egyptian, but the records are those of Abraham and Joseph, and contain important information respecting the creation, the fall of man, the deluge, the patriarchs, the book of Mormon, the lost tribe, the gathering, the end of the world, the judgment, &c. &c. This is as near as I can recollect; if there is an error I hope some of the Mormons will point it out, and I will recall it. These records were torn by being taken from the roll of embalming salve which contained them, and some parts entirely lost; but Smith is to translate the whole by divine inspiration, and that which is lost, like Nebuchadnezzar's dream, can be interpreted as well as that which is preserved; and a larger volume than the Bible will be required to contain them. For further account of these mummies and records, see Mormon Advocate, of December, 1835.

—William S. West, *A Few Interesting Facts Respecting the Rise and Progress and Pretensions of the Mormons,* pamphlet, 1837.

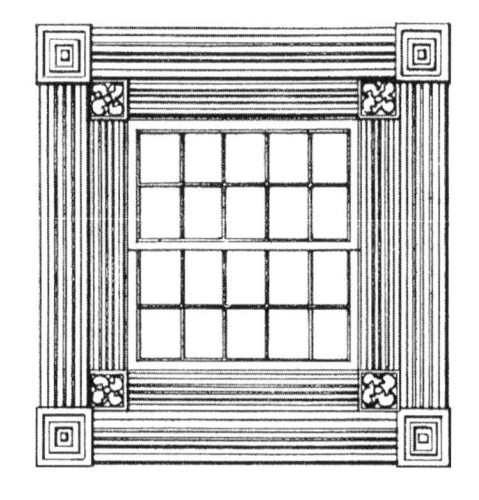

Exodus *of the* Saints

Joseph and Sidney flee Kirtland, by Henry K. Inoyuye Jr.

FROM ITS HIGHPOINT, surrounding the 1836 dedication of the Kirtland Temple, the church moved quickly into a period of financial instability and disruption. The failure of a speculative church banking enterprise, known as the Kirtland Safety Society Anti-Banking Co., tore apart stalwart bonds of friendship that had formerly characterized the fellowship. Support for church leaders disintegrated as members challenged one another over unpaid mortgages and mounting debts. Threats of legal action and personal violence resulted in the hasty departure of Joseph Smith and Sidney Rigdon and their families from Kirtland under cover of darkness.

Martin Harris remained a resident for thirty years after the departure of the Latter Day Saints. Fortunately, many interesting reminiscences shedding light on this less familiar period of Harris's career have been preserved.

John Smith, 1838

John Smith, Sr.

JOHN SMITH, JOSEPH Smith Jr.'s uncle, documented the excommunication of a number of LDS members who were no longer perceived as supportive of the direction of the church after Joseph's departure.

THE SPIRITUAL condition at this time is gloomy also. I called the High Council together last week and laid Before <them> the case of a com-pan<y> of Decenters [Dissenters] 28 persons where [were] upon after mature Discussion proceeded to cut them off from the chh [church]; the Leaders were Cyrus Smalling Joseph Coe Martin Harris Luke Johnson John Boynton and W[arren] W Parrish. we have cut off Between 40 & 50 from the Chh [Church] Since you Left...

—John and Clarissa Smith to George A. Smith, 1 January 1838, George A. Smith Papers, LDS Church Archives.

William McLellin

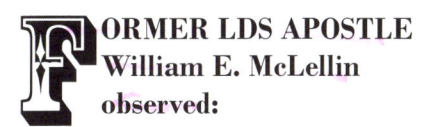

FORMER LDS APOSTLE William E. McLellin observed:

ABOUT SEVENTY OF Joseph [Smith]'s first elders quit him. Among them, the three "witnesses;" David, Oliver and Martin, his scribe and church recorder, his private secretary, a member of the twelve, and a number of his high councilors, &c., &c. The name was a matter of contention.

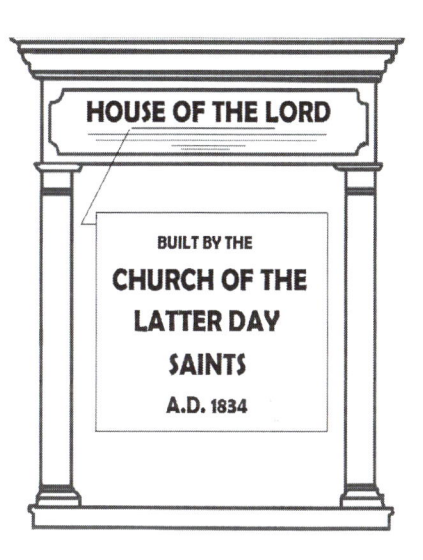

> HOUSE OF THE LORD
>
> BUILT BY THE
> CHURCH OF THE
> LATTER DAY
> SAINTS
> A.D. 1834

The dissenters took for their church the original name of the "Church of Christ," and Martin Harris furnished the money, and Leonard Rich went to Chardon, and got the name recorded. This alarmed the "Lick Skillets," and they got together, and changed the name to the "Church of Christ of L.D.S." Thus it remained until in Far West they added to it "Jesus," and so they have worn that name ever since.

—William E. McLellin, Independence, Missouri, to D. H. Bays, 24 May 1870, *Herald* 17, no. 18 (15 September 1870):553.

William E. McLellin

Church *of* Christ

SHORTLY AFTER Joseph Smith and Sidney Rigdon left Kirtland, a notice appeared on the Kirtland Temple, announcing a meeting of the "Church of Christ." In accordance with Ohio law, trustees were chosen and the original church name was incorporated, with Joseph Coe, Martin Harris, and Cyrus Smalling named as trustees. As recorded in Geauga County, Ohio, records:

STATE OF OHIO} Geauga County ss.}
Be it known that before me Warren A. Cowdery a Justice of the Peace in and for Kirtland Township in said County personally appeared Joseph Coe, Martin Harris & Cyrus Smalling and took the following oath to wit; You and each of you do swear in the presence of Almighty God, that you will support the Constitution of the United States and the constitution of the state of Ohio, and will faithfully discharge your duties as Trustees of the Church of Christ in Kirtland township in said County to the best of your abilities Kirtland Jany 18th. 1838. W. A. Cowdery, J.P.

State of Ohio} ss. To the Clerk of the Court of Common Geauga County} Pleas in said County. We the undersigned Trustees of the Church of Christ do certify under our hands & seals that we do recognize the name of the Church of Christ and that the above proceedings, have been had, and said Church is situated in Kirtland Township in said County.
 Joseph Coe [Seal]
 Martin Harris [Seal]
 Cyrus Smalling [Seal]
 Kirtland Jany 18, 1838

—Geauga County, Ohio, Execution Docket 1831-1835, microfilm # 1,289,257, item 1, Family History Library. See Christin Craft Mackay and Lachlan Mackay, "A Time of Transition: The Kirtland Temple, 1838-1880," *John Whitmer Historical Association Journal* 18 (1998): 133-48.

ON 25 MARCH 1838, the new group, under the leadership of Warren Parrish, ran into trouble in the Kirtland Temple. Several renounced the Book of Mormon, but Harris arose and testified that the book was true.

George A. Smith

JOSEPH SMITH'S cousin, George A. Smith, attended this service and reported:

LAST SABBATH [Sunday, 25 March 1838] A division arose amoung [among] the Par[r]ish party abou[t] the Book of mormon John Boyington[,] W[arren] Par[r]ish[,] L[uke] Johnson and others Said it was nonsense Martin Har[r]is then bore testimony of its truth and said all would [be] damned that rejected it C[yrus]. Smalling[,] J[oseph] Coe and others declaired [declared] his testimony was true.

—George A. Smith to Josiah and Nancy Flemming, 29-31 March 1838. Portion quoted written 29 March 1838, LDS Church Archives.

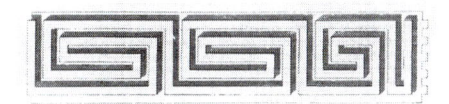

Stephen Burnett

STEPHEN BURNETT, AN elder who had publicly renounced Joseph Smith in the spring of 1838, also described the meeting:

...three week[s] since in the Stone Chapel [I] gave a full history of the church since I became acquainted with it, the false preaching & prophecying etc of Joseph [Smith] together with the reasons why I took the course which I was resolved to do, and renounced the Book of Mormon with the whole scene of lying and deception practiced by J[oseph]. S[mith] & S[idney]. R.[igdon] in this church, believ=ing as I verily do, that it is all a wicked deception palmed upon us unawares[.]

I was followed by W[arren]. Parish[,] Luke Johnson & John Boynton all of who concurred with me, after we were done speaking M[artin] Harris arose & said he was sorry for any man who rejected the Book of Mormon for he knew it was true, he said he had hefted the plates repeatedly in a box with only a tablecloth or a handkerchief over them, but he never saw them only as he saw a city through a mountain. And said that he never should have told that the testimony of the eight [witnesses] was false, if it had not been picked out of [h]im but should have let it passed as it was.

—Stephen Burnett, Orange Township, Geauga County, Ohio, to Lyman E. Johnson, 15 April 1838, Joseph Smith Letterbook, 2:64-66, Joseph Smith Papers, LDS Church Archives, as cited in Vogel, *Early Mormon Documents* 2:290-93.

Heber C. Kimball's Visit, 1839

THE SITUATION IN Kirtland remained troubled. Apostle Heber C. Kimball spent three weeks in Kirtland in November 1839. During a 10 November 1839 meeting, Kimball compared former members

...to a parcel of old earthen pots that were cracked in burning, for they were mostly apostates that were living there. Immediately after I returned to the house of Ira Bond; Martin Harris, Cyrus Smalling and others came in and attacked me on what I had been saying, asking me who I referred to in my comparisons; said I, "to no one in particular, but to anyone that the coat fits."

—History of Heber C. Kimball in Helen Mar [Kimball] Whitney, "Life Incidents," *Woman's Exponent* 9 (15 July 1880): 26, as cited in Richard and Jeni Holzapfel, eds., *A Woman's View: Helen Mar Whitney's Reminiscences of Early Church History* (Provo, Utah: Brigham Young University, Religious Studies Center, 1997), 25-26.

Heber C. Kimball

Return *to* Fellowship, 1838

BY JULY 1840, Harris was fellowshipping again in Kirtland with others who were supportive of Smith's leadership. In May 1839, LDS leaders meeting at Quincy, Illinois, decided to build up Kirtland again. Conference adopted a resolution encouraging the Saints living in the eastern states to "Move to Kirtland and the vicinity thereof, and again settle that place as a Stake of Zion." The same resolution appointed Oliver Granger to preside over the Kirtland Church and to take charge of the House of the Lord. As a result, by the end of 1839, a small Mormon congregation was meeting in the Temple. However, leaders in Illinois needed members to buy land in Nauvoo to help relieve church debt. An epistle from the First Presidency, dated December 1839, warned the brethren [in the west] "in the name of the Lord, not to remove [to Kirtland]."

—*History of the LDS Church*, 3:345 and 4:45.

Almon Babbitt, 1840

DURING THE October 1840 conference in Nauvoo, Illinois, Joseph Smith sent Almon W. Babbitt to preside over the church at Kirtland. Under Babbitt, the church in Kirtland experienced explosive growth. Throughout this period, Martin remained attached to the church. On 18 July 1840, Laura Pitkin advised Heber C. Kimball from Nauvoo:

> **B**ROTHER Joseph [Smith] received a letter from Kirtland last week. Martin Harris has come into the church. Oliver Cowdery is very friendly and [they] have pro[s]perous times in that place.
>
> —Laura Pitkin to Heber C. Kimball, 18 July [1840], published in Kate B. Carter, comp., *Heart Throbs of the West* 5 (Salt Lake City: Daughters of Utah Pioneers, 1944):382.

Almon W. Babbitt by Anne Romig.

BY MAY 1841, around 350 in the Kirtland area were aligned with Joseph Smith. The 22 May 1841 Kirtland Conference minutes included Martin Harris as a member of the high priests Quorum. In May 1841, members also incorporated in Ohio as the "Church of Christ of Latter Day Saints."

—*Times and Seasons* 2:458; Milton V. Backman, Jr., *The Heavens Resound* (Salt Lake City: Deseret Book, 1983), 140.

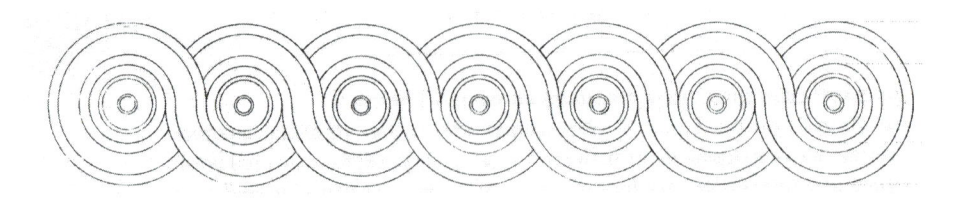

1841 Obituary

MARTIN RECEIVED AN unusual tribute in the form of an obituary written thirty-four years before his death. Upon receiving word that Harris had died, Alvah Strong, a Rochester, New York, editor, wrote this description of his former acquaintance:

WE HAVE EVER regarded Mr. Harris as an honest man. We first became acquainted with him at Palmyra, in the spring of 1828, shortly after the plates from which the Book of Mormon is said to have been translated, were found.... Though illiterate and actually of a superstitious turn of mind, he had long sustained an irreproachable character for probity.... By his neighbors and townsmen with whom he earnestly and almost incessantly labored, he was regarded rather as being deluded himself, than as wishing to delude others knowingly; but still he was subjected to many scoffs and rebukes, all of which he endured with a meekness becoming a better cause."

—*Rochester Daily Democrat*, 23 June 1841, cited in Anderson, 101-02.

Editors note: This misunderstanding was quickly corrected by the Painesville *Telegraph*.

Rebaptism, 1842

HARRIS ASKED for rebaptism when Apostle Lyman Wight visited Kirtland in 1842. Wight chaired a conference at Kirtland on 31 October and 1 November 1842. Harris was among 203 persons baptized within a four-day period. LDS member Justin Brooks advised, "Twelve persons were baptized yesterday and information has just reached me that Brother Martin Harris has been baptized."

—Justin Brooks to Joseph Smith, 7 November 1842, Journal History, LDS Church Archives.

ANOTHER member, Jacob Scott, observed, "Martin Harris, one of the 3 Special witnesses, has been baptized and admitted again into the Church; and scores of other Dissenters."

—Jacob Scott, Nauvoo, Illinois, 28 February 1843, P12-1, f5, CofChrist Archives.

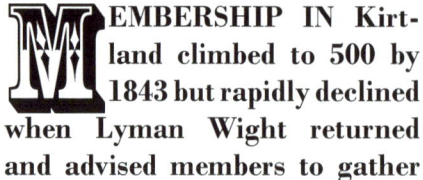

MEMBERSHIP IN Kirtland climbed to 500 by 1843 but rapidly declined when Lyman Wight returned and advised members to gather to Nauvoo.

—*Times and Seasons* 4 (1 August 1843):284.

Martin *and the* Shakers, 1844

MARTIN'S reconcilliation was short lived. During the vacuum created by the LDS gathering at Nauvoo, Harris turned his religious attention elsewhere. By 1844 Martin had become attracted by local spiritual manifestations occurring in Shaker communities nearby. Martin became a follower of the teachings of Mother Ann Lee, founder of the Shaker movement. In 1844, Phineas Young wrote to his brother Brigham Young and the Twelve Apostles in Nauvoo:

Kirtland, Dec. 31, 1844

Beloved Brethren:
In as much as an important cricis [crisis] is at hand, in relation to the Church of Jesus Christ of Latter Day Saints and its future destiny, we the undersigned, feeling a great desire for the prosperity of Zion feel it a duty to apprise you of the situation of the church in this part of the Lords vineyard. We have long looked for the redemption of Zion. Our eyes have failed for watching while those who have control over us here have caused us to weep and mourn. Our beloved prophet has found rest in the paradise of God, our Patriarch has finished his work and we now see a fulfillment of that which was told you last winter. The work (says Bro. Joseph) rests upon your shoulders. Consequently, we appeal to you. There are in this place all kinds of teaching, Martin Harris is a firm believer in Shakerism, says his testimony is greater than it was of the Book of Mormon. Luman Heath is running after them continually. Hiram Kellog, the presiding officer here is a Rigdonite and says Sidney is the man God had called to lead his people; that Bro. Joseph was cut off for transgression and the Twelve are carrying out his principles; and if we follow them, we shall all be cut off. He is also an agent for the "Messenger and Advocate" printed in Pittsburg, and no pain is spared by him to circulate it among our worst enemies. He will take his seat in the Holy desk and there dictate with unbounded sovereignty [to] every

Shakers Dancing

person who attempts to speak, and then at the close of the service distribute the Rigdon papers. Was this the first signs of apostasy in Hiram Kellog, we could bear with him for awhile; but when our brethren were in prison in Missouri, he said it was by reason of the wickedness of Bro. Joseph. These things are all provable, and we felt in duty bound to lay them before you. We said we had long looked for the redemption of Zion. We still look for that glorious day and feel to bear record that if we carry out the principles taught by Bro. Joseph, we shall share in its triumphs; but we have a double portion at the present time in this place, for here we are called Josephites, and at Nauvoo apostates; the first we glory in, the latter we are willing to bear till our brethren shall have proven us faithful by seeing our faith and good works. There are at this time some 40 or 50 good brethren in this place, which constitutes a majority of the Church here, and we are anxious to have them saved, if possible, but we are at our wits end, having every kind of spirit to deal with, but we are favored with the house [Kirtland Temple] and the control of it. Old Burness had returned the keys to Bro. Hiram Winters.

We would say in relation to tithing, we are willing to do all we can and intend to make out our tenth as early in the spring as possible, and forward it to the Trustees-in-Trust for the building of the Lord's house that we may not be behind in any one thing.

We would say to our brethren, the Twelve, dispose of us as you think proper, and for you we will ever pray. Phineas H. Young, J. Knight, Hiram Winters, Ira Tuft

To: Brigham Young

—Phineas H. Young, Jeremiah Knight, Hiram Winters, and Ira Tuft, Kirtland, Ohio to Brigham Young, 31 December 1844, Journal History, 31 December 1844, LDS Church Archives; see also Robert F. W. Meader, "The Vision of Brother Philemon [Stewart]," *Shaker Quarterly* 10 (Spring 1970):8-10.

Death *of* Joseph Smith, 1844

MORMON Missionaries in the eastern United States were alarmed by news of the death of President Joseph Smith Jr. on 27 June 1844 in the Carthage Jail, Carthage, Illinois.

On Monday the 24th inst., after Governor Ford had sent word, that those eighteen persons demanded on a warrant, among whom were Joseph Smith and Hyrum Smith, should be protected by the militia of the State, they in company with some ten or twelve others, started for Carthage.... About six o'clock in the afternoon the guard was surprised by an armed Mob of from 150 to 230... which poured a shower of bullets into the room where the unfortunate men were held....

—*The Prophet* 1, no. 10 (20 July 1844).

THROUGHOUT THE period surrounding Joseph Smith's death, Martin's religious aspirations were focused on Shaker matters. Meanwhile, LDS faithful convened a conference in the Kirtland Temple on 5 April 1845.

Sidney Rigdon

Sidney Rigdon, 1845

RIGDON'S reappearance in Kirtland could not reignite Harris's interest in Mormonism. In February 1845, Sidney preached in the Temple three times. But his movement quickly faded.

Other Leaders

THE TEMPLE remained nearly unused throughout 1845. Then S. B. Stoddard, Jacob Bump, Hiram Kellogg, and Jewell Raney broke into the House of the Lord and took possession. These individuals were able to retain control of the building for several years.

Kirtland Temple, as drawn by Henry Howe, 1846

James Strang, 1846

JAMES J. STRANG AND William B. Smith came to Kirtland in 1846 proclaiming Strang as Joseph Smith Jr.'s successor. Martin Harris was among those attracted by Strang's declaration of authority. Stoddard, Bump, Kellogg, and Raney also affiliated with Strang and made the Kirtland Temple available for his use. Strang held a conference in the Temple and reorganized Kirtland as a stake. During this conference, Martin Harris was installed as one of Strang's Kirtland Stake High Council. Strang's periodical, the *Voree Herald*, published the conference minutes:

> A CONFERENCE was held at Kirtland on the 7th, 8th, 9th and 10th of August [1846] and the Stake at that place reorganized according to the Law of the Lord and the word of his prophets.
>
> The attendance was very general, nearly all the branches in Northern Ohio being represented. President Strang presided—Lester Brooks was ordained an Apostle of the Lord Jesus Christ, Lester Brooks and Moses Smith of the Twelve, and Martin Harris and Hazen Aldrich, High-priests with several Elders were appointed to go to England. A full set of officers of the stake were appointed, and a most perfect state of union produced.
>
> The Saints in Kirtland are in full legal and peaceable posses-

James J. Strang

sion of the Temple of God in that place. They hold it by legal title. The usurpers have brought a suit against them, and after preparing the cause for trial they withdrew the suit and paid up the cost leaving the true Church in possession of the Temple. Moreover the organization includes nearly every person in Kirtland who held a standing in any of the parties into which the Church has been divided. . . .

Resolved, That we sustain and uphold with our faith and prayers, and acknowledge in his administration James J. Strang, as First President of this Church, and as the duly appointed successor to Joseph Smith, as Prophet, Seer, Revelator and Translator unto this Church, according to the Law of the Church, and the word of God. . . .

The Presidency consists of Leonard Rich, Amos Babcock and Sylvester B. Stoddard, and Jacob Bump as Bishop.

—*Voree Herald* 1, no. 9 (September 1846):1.

But Strang did not retain possession of the Temple for long.

Mission *to* England

MARTIN BEGAN preparing for his mission to England within a month of Strang's conference. Harris assigned power of attorney to his brother Preserved and to Jacob Bump who served as the group's bishop. Martin planned to travel to Great Britain with **Apostle Lester Brooks, Moses Smith, and Hazen Aldrich.** The mission was expected to last one year. Harris wrote:

> Kirtland Sept the 4th 1846
> KNOW ALL MEN BY these presents that I Martin Harris am about to leav[e] this Continut [Continent] and expect to go to Europe and remain there one year or more. I therefore constitute Jacob Bump and Preserved Harris my lawful

Sailing for England

agents to transact all my business in my name and I do further mor[e] giv[e] the said Bump and Harris the full care and controll [sic] of my farm and all my personal property in the township of Kirtland and for the benefit of my family and the Church of Christ of which I am a member It is further understood that the said Jacob Bump and Preserved Harris is [to] hold there [sic] agency for at least one year and if I do not return within one year their agency to continue until my return. And I hereby this day, by these presents deliver to the said Bump & Harris all the cattle—sheep—grain—hogs—family utensils for this use abov[e] mentioned with the right to work or lease my farm as my agents shall think proper—

Signed sealed day and year above mentioned In presence of—

Nathaniel Milliken
Martin Harris
Wm H Fuller

—Martin Harris, Power of Attorney, Lake County Historical Society.

HARRIS ARRIVED IN England in October 1846. But LDS apostles Orson Hyde and John Taylor preceded him and prepared a hot reception. Orson Hyde cautioned British members to be wary of Martin Harris.

We understand that he is appointed a mission to this country, but we do not feel to warn the Saints against him, for his own unbridled tongue will soon show out specimens of folly enough to give any person a true index to the character of the man....

—Orson Hyde, "Notices," *Millennial Star* 8 (15 November 1846):128.

Harris returned from England on the Ship Sea.

THE LACK OF THE mission's success cut the trip short and Harris returned to the United States. Lester Brooks accompanied Martin back to the United States and left Harris in Pittsburgh, Pennsylvania. James Smith of Pittsburgh informed Strang about Harris's return.

THIS MAN, ALTHOUGH he has been buffeted and scoffed at by the world made our hearts glad in consequence of the unwavering testimony which he bore with regard to the origin of Mormonism.

—James Smith to James J. Strang, no date, circa January 1847, *Zion's Reveille* 2 (11 February 1847): 18.

Orson Hyde

WHEN MARTIN returned to Kirtland, he learned that Leonard Rich and others had rejected James Strang's leadership. But Harris found William Fuller in possession of Martin's farm. Harris filed suit against Fuller and Bishop Jacob Bump in an unsuccessful attempt to regain control of his farm. The jury found the defendant "not guilty as complained against him," except for a small half acre of land.

—Martin Harris Legal Documents, L. Tom Perry Special Collections Library, Brigham Young University.

William McLellin

NO SOONER HAD Martin Harris left Strang's group when William E. McLellin appeared in town touting David Whitmer as the legitimate church president. McLellin based this claim upon Joseph Smith's 1834 ordination of David Whitmer in Clay County, Missouri. McLellin believed Smith had ordained David to be his successor.

McLellin's followers gained access to the Temple and held a conference on 23 January 1847. Conference minutes appear in McLellin's Kirtland-based periodical, the *Ensign of Liberty* contains the conference minutes:

David Whitmer

THE ENSIGN OF LIBERTY,
OF THE CHURCH OF CHRIST.

VOL. I. - - - - - - KIRTLAND, LAKE COUNTY, OHIO, APRIL, 1847. - - - - - - NO. 2.

AFTER MANY remarks by those present, it was motioned by W. E. McLellin, and seconded by Martin Harris, that this church take upon them the name of the Church of Christ, and wear it henceforth—shorn of all appendages or alterations. The motion was put by Elder Leonard Rich, the chairman, and carried with much feeling and spirit, in the affirmative—without a dissenting voice.

—"The Name of the Church," *The Ensign of Liberty* 1 (April 1847): 20.

WILLIAM E. McLellin, hoping to attract others to the new movement, published regular reports in *The Ensign of Liberty*:

ON THE 10TH OF Feb.... we felt troubled in our minds about our baptisms and confirmations.... All who had been baptized and confirmed by any and all the Elders under Joseph [Smith, Jr.] after he had ordained his Successor, consequently had no more power with God in his station....

—"Things in Kirtland," *The Ensign of Liberty* 1, no. 4 (January 1848): 54-55.

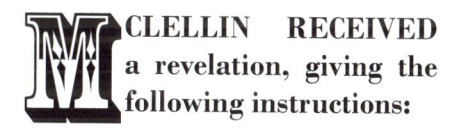

McLELLIN RECEIVED a revelation, giving the following instructions:

YEA, LET MY servant William [McLellin] baptize and confirm, and then re-ordain my [servant] Martin [Harris]. And thus shall he confirm his authority upon him by the laying on of hands and saying, Brother Martin I lay my hands upon you in the name of Jesus Christ, and I re-ordain you, and confirm upon you the office of high priest in the church of Christ, after the holy order of the Son of God. And I pray God in the name of Jesus, his son, to give unto you in your calling, all the gifts and blessings and powers thereof, and keep you faithful unto the end, amen.

And then let my servant Martin administer unto my servant William [McLellin] in the same manner, according to the same pattern. And then let my servant Leonard [Rich] likewise receive the same ministration. Yea, let my servants William and Martin and Leonard, do as the spirit of truth now directs them.

—"Our Tour West in 1847," *The Ensign of Liberty* 1, no. 7 (August 1849):100-101.

AS A RESULT OF THIS revelation, Martin was baptized and confirmed a member of McLellin's group on 13 February 1847. Harris was also re-ordained to the same authority which he "held in the Church before Latter Day Saintism was known."* McLellin's church numbered about forty-two members. The *Ensign* reported:

MARTIN HARRIS has retired to his little farm, in Kirtland, Ohio, and stands warning all, that the Church will not prosper until they throw away their fictitious name, and take again, as in the beginning, the NAME of "the Church of Christ."

—"A Special Conference," *Ensign of Liberty* 1, no. 1 (March 1847):11.

*The church changed its name from the Church of Christ to the Church of the Latter Day Saints in 1834. Martin had been ordained a high priest before the name change.

BUT BRIGHAM Young's followers were not willing to relinquish control of the Temple without confrontation. Almon Babbitt, the LDS agent, attempted to sell the temple, "a difficult task since the structure was not in his possession." While preaching in New York Babbitt claimed to have sold the Temple for ten thousand dollars. The deal fell through.

—J. Tyler to W. E. McLellin, February 1847, *Ensign of Liberty* 1, no. 4 (January 1848):60. See Christin Mackay and Lachlan-Mackay, "The Kirtland Temple," *JWHA Journal* 18 (1998):139.

The key to the Kirtland Temple was highly sought after.

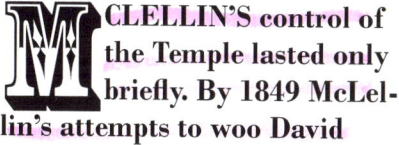

MCLELLIN'S control of the Temple lasted only briefly. By 1849 McLellin's attempts to woo David Whitmer failed and enthusiasm for his Church of Christ waned.

MARTIN'S PERSONAL circumstances deteriorated during this period.

IN 1849 KIRTLAND Township trustees provided $2.25 to Martin Harris for "poor purposes."

—Kirtland Township Records, [March] 1849, CofChrist Archives.

IN THE FALL OF 1849, Harris traveled to Rochester, New York where his visit was reported in a local newspaper:

HE [MARTIN] wrote the Book of Mormon from Joe Smith's dictation, the latter reading the text from the Golden Plates by putting his face in a hat.... But he no longer goes with the Mormons, saying that they "have gone to the devil just like other people." He abandoned them fifteen years ago, when they assumed the appellation of "Latter Day Saints," and bore his testimony against them by declaring that "Latter Day Devils" would be a more appropriate designation. Mr. Harris visited England some three years ago. At present he professes to have a mission from God, in fulfi[ll]ment of which he wanders about preaching to "all who will feed him." When this essential condition is not performed by his hearers, he shakes o[f]f the dust from his feet and leaves for more hospitable quarters. Mr. H. is exceedingly familiar with the Scripture[s], and discourses theology in his peculiar way.

—*Rochester* [New York] *Daily American* (November 16, 1849).

James Brewster

JAMES COLIN Brewster, the boy prophet, began receiving revelations in 1837 at age ten. Austin Cowles and Hazen Aldrich started a periodical on Brewster's behalf at Kirtland in August 1848. Brewster's Church of Christ gained access to the Temple by 1849. But the cost of heating the building during the winter prevented a group like this, with limited resources, from worshiping there on a regular basis.

James Bay, 1850

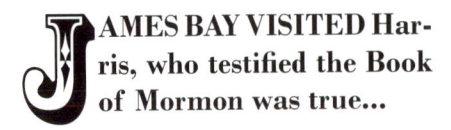

JAMES BAY VISITED Harris, who testified the Book of Mormon was true...

... for he saw the plates and knew for himself.... I read some in what they Called the Holy roll* but [found] no God.... I staid at Martins all night had quite a talk with him he thought that the 12 was [w]rong but I told him that he was [w]rong and he had better come up to the valley and see for himself."

—James Willard Bay, Journal, 23 November 1850, written after July 1895, LDS Church Archives

---

*While at Kirtland Francis Gladden Bishop printed "A Proclamation from the Lord to His People, Scattered Throughout All the Earth." It was an 8.5x21 inch, double sided sheet intended to fulfill Zechariah's prophecy of a "Flying Roll" to go out over the earth, to herald the gathering of Israel.
 —Richard L. Saunders, "Francis Gladden Bishop," Roger D. Launius and Linda Thatcher, *Differing Visions* (Urbana, IL:University of Illinois Press, *1994),112*.

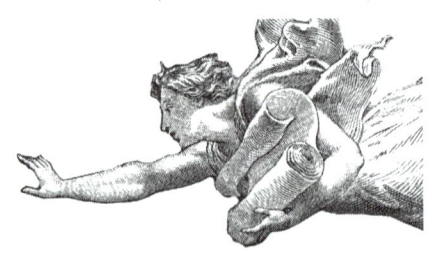

Reuben P. Harmon

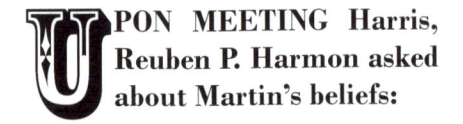

UPON MEETING Harris, Reuben P. Harmon asked about Martin's beliefs:

I WAS WELL acquainted with Martin Harris, who was often at my house for days at a time. I have questioned him much about the plates from which the "Book of Mormon" purports to have been translated. He never claimed to have seen them with his natural eyes, only spiritual vision. He said it was impossible for the prophet Joseph to get up the "Book of Mormon,"'for he could not spell the word Sarah. He had him repeat the letters of the word. He was a very illiterate man. He claimed he would be one of the 144,000 mentioned in Revelation and would not die but would be translated.

—Reuben P. Harmon, 16 December 1884, *Naked Truths about Mormonism* 1 (April 1888): 1. For Emma Smith statement about Sarah (Sariah) to Edmund C. Briggs, see Edmund C. Briggs, "A Visit to Nauvoo in 1856," *Journal of History* 9 (October 1916):454

Francis Gladden Bishop, 1851

IN THE FALL OF 1850, Francis Gladden Bishop came to Kirtland proclaiming himself a Mormon prophet. He attracted a few followers who conducted a meeting in the Temple, where on Sunday, 16 March 1851, Bishop delivered a description of the golden plates, the book of Ether, the Book of Life (the Sealed Record), the interpreters, the breast-plate of Moroni, and the sword of Laban:

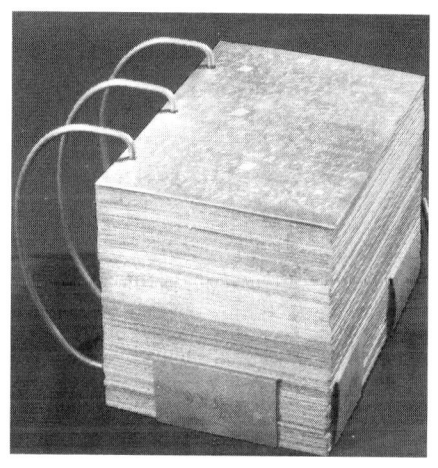

Plates as described by Witnesses

THE PLATES ARE pure gold; about eight inches in length, and about six inches in width, and in a compact form are about four inches in thickness, each plate being about the twelfth of an inch thick. There are in all forty-eight plates, divided as follows:— The first part, or division, consists of twenty-four plates—from these was the Book of Mormon translated; and on the first which stand as the Alphabet of the reformed Egyptian language, in which this whole division is written. The characters are rubbed over with a black substance so as to fill them up, in order that the dazzling of the gold between the characters would not prevent their being readily seen.

—Francis G. Bishop, Kirtland, Ohio, 6 April 1851, a broadside titled, "A Proclamation from the Lord to His People, Scattered Throughout all the Earth," LDS Church Archives

The Hill Cumorah

Ruben Alderman, 1852

RUBEN W. Alderman was a shoemaker from nearby Claridon, Geauga County, Ohio. In 1884 Arthur Buel Deming, an ardent anti-Mormon, interviewed Alderman hoping to expose early Mormonism.

IN FEBRUARY, 1852, I was snowbound in a hotel in Mentor, Ohio, all day. Martin Harris was there, and in conversation told me he saw Jo Smith translate the "Book of Mormon," with his peep-stone in his hat. Oliver Cowdery, who had been a school-teacher, wrote it down. Sidney Rigdon, a renegade preacher, was let in during the translation. Rigdon had stolen a manuscript from a printing office in Pittsburgh, Pa., which [Solomon] Spaulding, who had written it in the early part of the century, had left there to be printed, but the printers refused to publish it, but Jo and Rigdon did, as the "Book of Mormon." Martin said he furnished the means, and Jo promised him a place next to him in the church. When they had got all my property they set me out. He said Jo ought to have been killed before he was; that the Mormon[s] committed all sorts of depredations in the towns about Kirtland. They called themselves Latter-day Saints, but he called them Latter-day Devils.

[Signed.] R. W. ALDERMAN.
Witnessed by:
  Clara Alderman
  A. B. Deming
Claridon, Geauga Co., Ohio
Dec. 25, 1884.

—R. W. Alderman, Affidavit to Arthur B. Deming, 25 December 1884, *Naked Truths About Mormonism* 1 (January 1888):3. Biographical information about Deming, from Vogel, *Early Mormon Documents*, 2 (Salt Lake City: Signature Books, 1998), 185-87.

Spaulding Manuscript

Ruben McBride, 1852

RUBEN MCBRIDE returned to Kirtland in 1841 to assist with efforts to manage complicated financial matters. Ruben remained until 1852. When he left, the Kirtland Temple was in Mormon control.

IN THE YEAR 1841 at the fall conference held the 6th Oct at Nauvoo, Ill I Was appointed By Brother Joseph Smith in place of Oliver Grainger who Died in Kirtland Ohio and Recvd a general power of atty to transact Business in the Eastern and Middle States and more particularly Kirtland Lake Co Ohio and take charge of all the Church property in that place including the Temple the farm was rented to Joseph Coe who had left the Ch, in the Year 1844, I recvd a letter from Br Joseph to remove him from the farm Mr. Coe Refusing to pay the rent because he Said the Ch owed him for his share of the Egyptian Mummies and was not willing to leave the place I removed him and took possession of the place 15 April /44 in July/45 the Rigdonites tried to drive me by force off the place my life was threatened by Jacob Bump who once belonged to the Church through Mobbing and continual trouble by day and by night by Rigdonites and Strangites all apostates from the church and Law Suit after Law Suit about the farm also the Temple and House & Lot formerly the Carlos Smith House & Lot <I held it> until it was Quieted down by Law in 1847 in the Same fall I delivered up the farm to Almon W. Babbit [Babbitt] one of the Trustees of the Ch it was Sold for $ fifteen hundred Dollars Out of which I recvd 350, Dollars in property Such as Waggons Harness and Store goods Receipting the same to Babbit also Recvd the House and Lot the House being a mere Shell being on the Commons having the Expense of three Law Suits to get a man out of the House by the name of Lehasa Hollister who was in the house when Br Joseph was killed and refused to go out, at the time Called worth $100, by A. W. Babbit Trustee for the church. President Brigham Young said I could have this property to remove my family to Salt Lake Valley. By the Advise of Pres Young I left in 1852 with my family for Salt Lake Valley. Leaving the Temple in care of Christopher

Oliver Cowdery painted holding Egyptian Scroll, 1837

Dixon & Charles Parmer.... [This] Fulfilled the Prediction of Br Joseph which was if I would take a bold Stand my Enemies Should Suck up the very dust of my feet in Kirtland.

—Ruben McBride, Statement, MS 3171, LDS Church Archives.

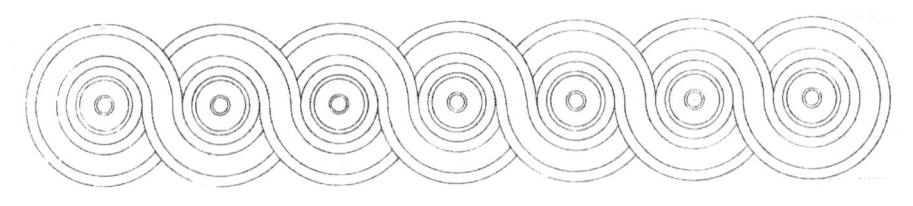

David Dille, 1853

DAVID BUEL DILLE was a Utah dairy farmer. In the spring of 1853, while on his way to England, Elder David Dille visited Martin Harris. He found Harris living about two miles east of Kirtland. Martin was bedfast, so sick that he had not eaten anything in three days. The seventy-two-year-old Harris insisted on getting dressed at once, ate a meal, and spent the rest of the day in animated conversation with the young missionary. Dille even heard Martin preach in the evening.

September 15, 1853

BE IT KNOWN TO all [to] whom this may come that I, David B. Dille, of Ogden City, Weber County, Salt Lake, en route to Great Britain, having business with one Martin Harris, formerly of the Church of Latter-day Saints, and residing at Kirtland, Lake County, Ohio, did personally wait upon him at his residence, and found him sick in bed; and was informed by the said Martin Harris that he had not been able to take any nourishment for the space of three days. This, together with his advanced age, had completely prostrated him. After making my business known to Mr. Harris, and some idle conversation with him, the said Martin Harris started up in bed, and after particularly inquiring concerning the prosperity of the Church, made the following declaration: "I feel that a spirit has come across me—the old spirit of Mormonism; and I begin to feel as I used to feel; and I will not say I won't go to the [Salt Lake] Valley." Then addressing himself to his wife, he said—"I don't know but that, if you will get me some breakfast, I will get up and eat it."

I then addressed Mr. Harris relative to his once high and exalted station in the Church, and his then fallen and afflicted condition. I afterwards put the following questions to Mr. Harris, to which he severally replied with the greatest cheerfulness. "What do you think of the Book of Mormon? Is it a divine record?" Mr. Harris replied and said—"I was the right hand man of Joseph Smith, and I know that he was a Prophet of God. I know the Book of Mormon is true." Then smiting his fist on the table he said—"And you know that I know that it is true. I know that the plates have been translated by the gift and power of God, for his voice declared it unto us; therefore I know of a surety that the work is true. For" continued Mr. Harris, "did I not at one time hold the plates on my knee an hour and a half, whilst in conversation with Joseph, when we went to bury them in the woods, that the enemy might not obtain them? Yes, I did. And as many of the plates as Joseph Smith translated I handled with my hands, plate after plate." Then describing their dimensions, he pointed with one of the fingers of his let hand to the back of his right hand and said, "I should think they were so long, or about eight inches, and about so thick, or about four inches; and each of the plates was thicker than the thickest tin."

I then asked Mr. Harris if he ever lost 3,000 dollars by the publishing of the Book of Mormon? Mr. Harris said—"I never lost one cent. Mr. Smith," he said, "paid me all that I advanced, and more too.'" As much as to say, he received a portion of the profits accruing from the sale of the book.

Mr. Harris further said—"I took a transcript of the characters of the plates to Dr. Anthon, of New York. When I arrived at the house of Professor Anthon, I found him in his office and alone, and presented the transcript to him, and asked him to read it. He said, if I would bring the plates, he would assist in the translation. I told him I could not, for they were sealed. Professor Anthon then gave me a certificate certifying that the characters were Arabic, Chaldaic, and Egyptian. I then left Dr. Anthon, and was near the door, when he said, "How did the young man know the plates were there?" said an angel had shown them to him. Professor Anthon then said, "Let me see the certificate!"– upon which, I took it from my waistcoat pocket and unsuspectingly gave it to him. He then tore it up in anger, saying there was no such thing as angels now—it was all a hoax. I then went to Dr. Mitchell with the transcript, and he confirmed what Professor Anthon had said."

Mr. Harris is about 58 years old and is on a valuable farm of 90 acres, beautifully situated at Kirtland, Lake County, Ohio.

—David B. Dille, "Additional Testimony of Martin Harris to the Coming Forth of the Book of Mormon," 15 September 1853, *Millennial Star* 21, no. 34 (20 August 1859):545-46.

Thomas Colburn, 1855

LDS MISSIONARY Thomas Colburn also interviewed Harris.

St. Louis, May 2, 1855.
ELDER SNOW, Editor of the *Luminary*:

Dear Brother—

At the conference held in St. Louis, in October, 1854, Brother W. W. Rust and myself received a mission to travel in the northern and eastern states, to hunt up the lost sheep and endeavor to gather them into the fold. . . .

We made it a rule to inquire for Saints and places to preach, but no sooner than we had informed them that we were ministers of the Gospel from Salt Lake, their doors were closed against us; we traveled hundreds of miles in Michigan, but obtained but one house to preach in. The fact is, Strang, the Beaver Island Mormon, as he styled himself, is sending his emissaries out to rob, steal, plunder, preaching another Gospel, but styling themselves Mormons; hence, the prejudice that exists in the minds of the people against the servants of God that are sent abroad by the authorities of The Church of Jesus Christ of Latter-day Saints.

We called at Kirtland, found a few that called themselves Saints, but very weak, many apostates, who had mostly joined the rappers [spiritualists]. We had a lengthy interview with Martin Harris. . . . He confessed that he had lost confidence in Joseph Smith, consequently his mind became darkened, and he was left to himself; he tried the Shakers, but they would not do, then tried Gladden Bishop, but no satisfaction; had concluded he would wait until the Saints returned to Jackson County, and then he would repair there. He gave us a history of the coming forth of the Book of Mormon; his going to New York and presenting the characters to Professor Anthon, etc., concluded before we left that "Brigham Young was Governor," and that he should go there as soon as he could get away.

—Thomas Colburn, to Elder Snow, editor, *St. Louis Luminary* (5 May 1855):2.

Martin Harris's Proclamation, 1855

IN MAY 1855, Martin Harris published a proclamation. It was purported to have been given by Moses, Elias, Elijah, and John "through a Miss Sexton a Spirit medium of Cleveland." The following extracts are from Harris's eight-page pamphlet titled, *A Proclamation and a Warning Voice unto All People, First to All Kings, Governors and Rulers in Authority, and unto Every Kindred Tongue and People Under the Whole Heavens, to Whom this Word Shall Come*:

A PROCLAMATION and a warning voice unto all people, first to all Kings, Governors and Rulers in Authority, and unto every kindred tongue and people under the whole heavens, to whom this word shall come, greeting:

Moses, Elias, Elijah and John set forth and declare the word of the Lord unto you... for behold this is the word of the proclamation that we, Moses, Elias, Elijah, and John have appeared unto many to declare unto them and now command it to be written and sent out unto all people....

And to my servant and friend whose name is held in sacred remembrance in the councils of the just, and who is called the messenger of the covenant, and who was first called among the sons of Ephraim to set forth in order the dispensation of the fullness [sic] of times—he it is to whom the key of knowledge has been given to go forth in the power of Elijah, and to bear off the ark of the Lord in wisdom and in power; for he shall be filled with light and his bowles [sic] shall be as a fountain of knowledge; and none shall gainsay or resist his words; nor shall he be confounded, and he shall divide the inheritance to the saints by lot, when Zion shall be established in the glory and power of her king.

And all who know the power and glory of this work of the gathering up of the sons of Israel for Zion and for the organization of the Church and house of the Lord, shall know this servant and messenger when they hear his voice, for he speaketh the words of Elijah, and is sent to do the work of Elijah, and feareth not to sacrifice, that the kingdom and the glory thereof might be one.

And this my servant is now standing in your midst, and ye know him not.... We come to administer to you in spirit, for our bodies are not yet risen from the dead; yet still we are bodies of spirit, or have spiritual bodies.

—Martin Harris, A Proclamation and a Warning Voice unto All People, First to All Kings, Governors and Rulers in Authority (Cleveland, 1855). Proclamation in LDS Church Archives.

Brigham Young

HARRIS ALSO SENT A copy of the Proclamation to Brigham Young. In an accompanying letter to Young, Harris wrote:

[E]nclosed I Send you A Proclamation as you will discover by reading it given by Moses, Elias, Elijah, and John—you no doubt will recollect of a favor asked of me—of the lone of Some money upon the ground of relationship and in the name of god. I now make an appeal to you in the name of god and Command you in the name of god to Publish the Revelation I send you in your deseret news or in some of your public Journals Published in the vall[e]y that the word and Commandment of the Proclamation may go to all the world.

—Harris to Young, 13 August 1855, written for Harris, emphasis and equal signs (=) omitted, Brigham Young Collection, LDS Archives; photo in *BYU Studies* 24 (Fall 1984): 427. The letter and proclamation were received on 26 November 1855.

{ Brigham Young did not distribute the proclamation. }

Stephen Post, 1855-56

A CONFERENCE convened in the Kirtland Temple with Martin Harris, William Smith, a Br. Atwood and wife and Sister Soule. Martin Harris was elected president. Chilion Daniels, Stephen Post, William Smith, and Hiram Stratton were also present. The body decided not to organize a church at that time. Post recorded the gathering in his journal:

BR. MARTIN Harris had published a proclamation purporting to be given By Moses, Elias, Elijah & John through a Miss Sexton a Spirit medium of Cleveland.] Wm. Smith got a revelation given through the same medium [he?] read to me the purport of which was that We Moses Elias Elijah & John again come unto you &c & go on to give directions to different elders about reorganizing the church and appointing them to select a place for the gathering of the saints fictitious names were used for those who were to be the actors in this thing.

—Stephen Post, Journal, 5 October 1855, LDS Church Archives.

Post returned to Kirtland in April 1856:

WENT TO Kirtland & put up with Ira Bond[.] Sunday 6. Preached twice in the school house near the temple. Staid [sic] with Dixon Martin Harris came after meeting and staid also 7 Monday passed the day with M. H. at Dixons, Strattons & Palmers writing a letter.... April 9 This morning I copied some revelations of H. H. Deam....

—Stephen Post, Journal, 5 and 6 April 1856, LDS Church Archives.

The Fox sisters are associated with the birth of Spiritualism at Hydenville, New York, 1848.

Alone Again

IN 1856, MARTIN'S WIFE, Caroline, and the children gathered to Utah. Harris remained in Kirtland. In his role as a minister, he performed a baptism on 24 April 1857. The *Painesville Telegraph* reported:

ELDER MARTIN Harris, of the Latter Day Saints, on Friday last, baptized a happy convert in the river, near the Geauga Mills.

—*Painesville Telegraph* 35 (30 April 1857): 3.

Baptism, by Anne Romig

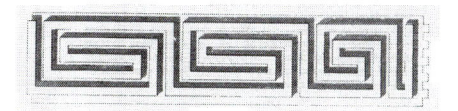

William Smith, 1857

William B. Smith

IN OCTOBER 1857, William B. Smith put in another appearance hoping "to organize as president in Kirtland."

—Davis Bitton, "The Warning of Mormon Kirtland," *BYU Studies* 12, no. 4 (Summer 1972):463. Stephen Post, Journal, 25 October 1857, LDS Church Archives.

Joel Tiffany, 1859

IN JANUARY 1859, Joel Tiffany, editor of *Tiffany's Monthly*, a Spiritualist publication, visited Martin Harris. Tiffany's account preserves Harris's recollection of events in Palmyra and Manchester, New York, prior to 1828:

WE WERE personally acquainted with Martin Harris, the real father of earthly Mormonism. He was the first associated with the Prophet Joseph Smith, and the one most intimate with him at the time the revelation commenced. Mr. Harris had conversed with us many times upon the subject, giving us the history of its earthly development, and desiring us to write it from his lips.... Mr. H[arris]. is a great expounder of the Bible, especially of all its dark sayings. He is the greatest stickler for its authenticity as the word of God; and lie proves to his own satisfaction, the genuineness of the Mormon Bible from it.

"Thus saith the Lord," is with Mr. H[arris]., the highest of all authority; and the end of all further question. He recognizes as of supreme authority, the letter of the Bible, only interpreting it by the Spirit of God that is upon him. His common expression when conversing upon the subject is, "the Lord showed me this," and "the Lord told me that." Observing that he frequently used such expressions, we inquired of him. How we were to understand the Lord showed him certain things, and in what manner He spake with him? He informed us that these revelations came by way of impression. That he was "impressed by the Lord." We suppose Mr. Harris speaks by the kind of influence and authority with which individuals since his revealments, have been "impressed to speak" and declare "mighty truths."

—Joel Tiffany, "Mormonism," *Tiffany's Monthly* 5 (May 1859):50-51.

MARTIN'S account clarifies his early association with the Joseph Smith family and the coming forth of the Book of Mormon:

THE FIRST TIME I heard of the matter, my brother Preserved Harris, who had been in the village of Palmyra, asked me if [I] had heard about Joseph Smith, jr., having a golden bible. My thoughts were that the money-diggers had probably dug up an old brass kettle, or something of the kind. I thought no more of it. This was about the first of October, 1827. The next day after the talk with my brother, I went to the village, and there I was asked what I thought of the Gold Bible?

. . . I then determined to go and see Joseph as soon as I could find time. A day or so before I was ready to visit Joseph, his mother came over to our house and wished to talk with me.[36]

I told her I had no time to spare, she might talk with my wife, and, in the evening when I had finished my work I would talk with her. When she commenced talking with me, she told me respecting his bringing home the plates, and many other things, and said that Joseph had sent her over and wished me to come and see him. I told her that I

Lucy Mack Smith, image ca. 1845

had a time appointed when I would go, and that when the time came I should then go, but I did not tell her when it was. I sent my boy to harness my horse and take her home. She wished my wife and daughter to go with her; and they went and spent most of the day.

When they came home, I questioned them about them. My daughter said, they were about as much as she could lift. They were now in the glass-box, and my wife said they were very heavy. They both lifted them. I waited a day or two, when I got up in the morning, took my breakfast, and told my folks I was going to the village, but went directly to old Mr. Smith's.

. . . While at Mr. Smith's I hefted the plates, and I knew from the heft that they were lead or gold, and I knew that Joseph had not credit enough to buy so much lead. I left Mr. Smith's about eleven o'clock and went home. I retired to my bedroom and prayed God to show me concerning these things, and I covenanted that if it was his work and he would show me so, I would put forth my best ability to bring it before the world. He then showed me that it was his work, and that it was designed to bring in the fullness of his gospel to the gentiles to fulfill his word, that the first shall be last and the last first. He showed this to me by the still small voice spoken in the soul. Then I was satisfied that it was the Lord's work, and I was under a covenant to bring it forth.

—Martin Harris to Joel Tiffany, "Mormonism—II," *Tiffany's Monthly* 5 (August 1859):166-70.

Francis M. Lyman

Francis Lyman, 1860

FRANCIS M. LYMAN was accompanied by Ruben A. McBride on a mission in England. Passing near Kirtland, they crossed Lake Erie in the steamboat *Ocean*. During the trip, Francis became seasick.

WE WENT TO Kirtland to visit the Temple and relatives. We were well received on every hand. Martin Harris took much pains to show us through the Temple. It was in a deplorable condition; as filthy as a stable, for it was used for dumb animals, and was also a rendezvous for the loafing whittlers, who had marred every appointment of beauty in the building. The lettering on the face of the pulpits had been cut out with the penknife. It was painful to see that sacred house so willfully desecrated. Brother Harris gave us all the information about the building that he could.

—Francis M. Lyman, June 1860, "My First Mission," *The Contributor* 17 (April 1896):352.

W. W. Blair, 1860

WILLIAM W. BLAIR, an apostle in the Reorganized Church, and James Blakeslee visited Kirtland in 1860. Blair noted in his journal:

> Wednesday Aug 8th [1860] ... Left Allegheny city for Cleveland... From Cleveland went to Willoughby... from Willoughby to Kirtland 3 miles where I am at this writing. Found Bro. Blakeslee all well He had been here near one week had preached a number of times and quite an interest is manifest among the Old Saints also with some of the Gentiles.

THE VISITORS MET with Martin Harris, Leonard Rich, and the James Twist family. At this time Zadock Brooks, Russell Huntley, and others controlled the Temple. So Blair and Blakeslee arranged to preach in the Kirtland Academy Hall instead. Blair continued:

> Thursday 9th Aug [1860] **L**AST NIGHT I WENT to prayer meeting at the Widow Daytons. Martin Harris, Leonard Rich & eight or ten others were present This day visited different ones of the Church among them James Twist & wife who were "waiting for the consolation of Israel" Yesterday recd one letter from my wife & one from Bro I. L. Rogers. Kirtland is a Sorry looking town yet it is a pretty Situation and is Surrounded by a good country of farming lands which are worth from $20 to $50 Dolls per acre. The Temple is in a Sad condition its walls inside and all its inside work Sadly defaced. The curtains for dividing of the main part into different appartments [sic] are taken away. I learn that Russell

Huntley [sic] designs fitting it up. If well done it will cost about $2000. Elder Z. Brooks, L. Rich & Martin Harris have formed an organization of 7 Souls 4 of them are women.

Sunday 12th [August 1860] R. B. PREACHED at ½ past 10 A.M. & myself at ½ past 2 PM in the Temple. Elder L. Rich at the close of afternoon services rather opposed us.

—W. W. Blair, Journal, 14 January-6 September 1860, J2, CofChrist Archives.

W. W. Blair, 1860

ON SUNDAY EVENING, the 19th of August [1860], Blair and Blakeslee attended a meeting in the Temple. Blair narrated what happened next:

Simeon Atwood, of Erie, Pennsylvania, and Leonard Rich, of Kirtland, were the speakers. By their request Elder Blakeslee and myself took seats in the stand with them and Martin Harris.

Elder Atwood was a member of the Brighamite Church.... He in a few moments sat down. Upon this a tall, long-haired, blue-eyed, ashy-complexioned, but well dressed man... arose and asked what practical thing they [the Mormons] proposed doing.

Leonard Rich rose up and replied with stentorian voice, and sought to set forth his views of what should be done. At this juncture the long-haired stranger sprang to his feet, uttered an unearthly yell, hissed, stamped his feet, shook his head, and looked like the embodiment of evil.

Mr. Rich at once dropped into his seat, and the stranger sprang upon the partition between the seats, came to the front, facing the stand, stamping, hissing, and making other violent demonstrations.

Pulpits in the Lower Court of the Temple.

Martin Harris, who sat on my left, whispered to me, saying, "I guess he has got the devil in him."

Feeling assured that the man would leap upon the stand... I slipped out on the right side of the stand, Brother Blakeslee moving out from the east end at the same moment, and immediately, at one bound, the stranger sprang squarely upon the speaker's desk, Harris, Rich, and Atwood leaving it with haste; and with another spring he reached the second stand, with another the third stand, and with still another the fourth and highest stand, this being on the Melchisedec Priesthood side of the temple. On reaching this highest point, he turned and faced the frightened, fleeing congregation, and stripping off his broadcloth coat, tearing it in strings and shreds, he again stamped and hissed and shook his head, swinging his torn coat and shouting to the people repeatedly. "Now is come the time of your trial!"

He then sprang down from one stand to the other and last, and then onto the partition between the seats in the body of the Temple, on which he ran across [to] the Aaronic priesthood side... and then, with a hiss, he thrust forward his right hand toward some ladies who were seeking exit at the door into the vestibule. Upon this a young lady, Miss Whitley, a school-teacher, who we learned had been a spiritual medium, fell prostrate and apparently lifeless upon the floor....

Looking out upon the people, a large number of them were in tears and all seemed filled with astonishment and consternation. Stepping down upon the street, we turned and saw the before mentioned stranger, his ragged coat rolled up and tucked under his arm, striding down the steps and then down the street in an excited way, after which we saw him no more. Upon inquiry we learned that he was a prominent spiritual medium, resided in New York, and that his name was—[Increase] Van Deusen.*

—Frederick B. Blair, comp., *The Memoirs of President W. W. Blair* (Lamoni, Iowa: Herald Publishing House, 1908), 35-38.

Kirtland Temple Pulpits, by Mather.

---

* Increase Van Dusen was fifty-one years old. In 1847 he published an account of the endowment ceremony performed in the Nauvoo Temple. He had recently moved with his wife Maria to Kirtland. See Craig L. Foster, "From Temple Mormon to Anti-Mormon: The Ambivalent Odyssey of Increase Van Dusen," *Dialogue* 27 (Fall 1994): 275-86.

James Blakeslee

Blair Interview

WHILE IN KIRTLAND, William W. Blair also interviewed Martin Harris. Blair indicated that, in response to direct inquiries, Harris personally related the story of the disappearance of the 116 manuscript pages of the Book of Mormon from his own lips:

HE [HARRIS] told the writer, in 1860, all the leading circumstances connected with the theft. Mr. Harris, by much persuasion, obtained them from Joseph in order to read to his wife, and to some very pious (?) friends who were at the time visiting at his house, whom he hoped to benefit by showing them the manuscript. Before retiring for the night he took the manuscript and put it in a bureau drawer, and locked the drawer; he then locked the parlor in which the bureau was, putting both keys in his pocket. This was the last he ever saw of the manuscript.

—W. W. Blair, "'Mormonism' Reviewed," *Herald* 23, no. 4 (15 February 1876):106-7; see also footnote by W. W. Blair, Lucy [Mack] Smith, *Biographical Sketches of Joseph Smith the Prophet, and His Progenitors for Many Generations* (Plano, Illinois: Reorganized Church of Jesus Christ of Latter Day Saints, 1880), 131.

W. W. Blair, ca. 1880

David Cannon, 1861

DAVID HENRY Cannon was born on 23 April 1838 in Liverpool, England. His parents, George Cannon and Ann Quayle Cannon, of the Isle of Man, joined the LDS Church in 1840. David Cannon visited Martin Harris while returning to Salt Lake City from a mission to England.

WHILE EAST I had some time on my hands so I went to Kirtland and called on Martin Harris, who was one of the witnesses to the Book of Mormon. He took me into the Kirtland Temple and I read to him his testimony as contained in the Book of Mormon, and I asked him if there was any possibility of him having been deceived in regard to the visitation of an angel. He testified to me in all solemnity, although not a member of the Church at that time, that the angel did appear with the plates from which the Book of Mormon was translated, and testified that they contained a history of the ancient inhabitants of this continent, and that they had been translated by the gift and power of God. There was a feeling [that] accompanied his testimony, when he bore it, that I have never experienced either or since in any man that I ever heard bear testimony.

—Beatrice Evans and Janath R. Cannon, *Cannon Family Historical Treasury* (Salt Lake City: George Cannon Family Association, 1967), 250; see also http://members.aol.com/cballd/cannon.html.

David H. Cannon

James McKnight, 1862

IN FEBRUARY 1862, James McKnight received a visit from Martin Harris. McKnight wrote of this brief visit:

WHILE AT Kirtland, a few days since, Martin Harris, one of the Three Witnesses of the Book of Mormon, came to see me. If any wish ocular demonstration of the fact that Joseph Smith is a prophet of God, they need only look at Martin Harris in his present state, and then read the words given through the martyred Joseph concerning him. He is failing perceptibly. Of his property there is little or none left. He has now no home; his son [George], a worthless scape-grace, with whom he lived, being in prison, and the house deserted. Yet, as you have doubtless often heard, he has never failed to confirm his testimony of the truth of that Book. He says he is going to Utah as soon as the Lord will release him. . . .

—James McKnight to George Q. Cannon, 27 February 1862, *Millennial Star* 24 (19 April 1862):251.

THE KIRTLAND Temple was sold in 1862 in hopes of settling Joseph Smith Jr's estate. Following its purchase by Russell Huntley, Zadock Brooks' "Church of Christ" met there regularly through 1864.

—Christin Mackay and Lachlan Mackay, 142.

Stephen Post, 1864

When Stephen Post visited Kirtland in 1864, he found members of the Reorganized Church worshiping together.

March 15 [1864] I came to Kirtland by rail R to Willoughby I tarried through the night with James Twist

16 Snowy I continued to stay with Br Twist he is united with Joseph Smith the youngers organization

18th. . . The Brooks party I learned have possession of the temple. It has been newly roofed a lightening rod put on it the old inscription on its east front chiseled out and a new one substituted reading thus "The house of the Lord built by the Church of Christ 1834. The former inscription being "The House of the Lord built by the Church of Jesus Christ [sic] of Latter Day Saints A.D. 1834."

—Stephen Post, Journal, 1864, LDS Church Archives.

Joseph Smith III, 1866

JOSEPH SMITH III preached in the Temple while passing through Kirtland in 1866. Of this visit, Smith noted:

THE TEMPLE IS IN tolerable repair, so far as the outside is concerned, but the inside has become the prey of the despoiler. All the ornamentation, moldings, letters, and carved works have been broken up by curiosity hunters, until the two upper rooms are stripped. It is in charge of Uncle Robert Greenough, who is trying to keep it from receiving further damage. How mankind can give way to such a spirit of vandalism is quite a mystery.

—Quoted in Vida E. Smith, *Young People's History* Vol. 2 (Lamoni, Iowa: Herald Publishing House, 1918), 129.

Joseph Smith III

Christopher Crary

LIFE BECAME MORE of a struggle for Martin Harris during the 1860s. Christopher G. Crary, a long-time resident of Kirtland and township trustee, described Harris's circumstances:

IN 1867 OR 1868, while acting as township trustee, complaint was made to me that Martin Harris was destitute of a home, poorly clothed, feeble, burdensome to friends, and that he ought to be taken to the poor-house. I went down to the flats to investigate, and found him at a house near the Temple, with a family lately moved in, strangers to me. He seemed to dread the poorhouse very much. The lady of the house said she would take care of him while their means lasted, and I was quite willing to postpone the unpleasant task of taking him to the poor-house. Everybody felt sympathy for him. He was willing to work and made himself useful as far as his age and debility would admit of.

—Christopher G. Crary, *Pioneer and Personal Reminiscences*, 44–45.

Martin Harris, ca. 1870, courtesy LDS Church Archives.

George Morse

George Morse, a Kirtland resident, recalled:

When I was a small boy Martin Harris, one of the witnesses of the Book of Mormon, was quite a frequent visitor to our house.... He was in destitute circumstances and used to visit around among the people, stopping several days at a time among different families.

—*Willoughby Republican* (29 June 1921).

Stephen Hart

MARTIN began visiting neighbouring communities in search of his livelihood. Stephen H. Hart, a resident of Mentor, Ohio, related the following to Arthur Deming:

MARTIN HARRIS, who furnished the money to pay for publishing the "Book of Mormon," worked off and on for fifteen or twenty years for me. His judgment about farming was good. When we had finished hoeing the corn he would raise his hands toward the field and pronounce a blessing and say he was sure of a good crop with his blessing. One night he went upstairs to bed without a light, but soon came down and said the devil had stirred his bed. My wife went upstairs with the light and found that the bed was all right; Martin said the devil had made it all right. There was a pile of bedding we supposed he had felt of instead of the bed. One night he fell down-stairs; he said the devil came to his bed and he had a tussle with him and the devil threw him down-stairs. Every wrong he attributed to the devil.

Martin claimed he would renew his age and be translated like Enoch. He said people would provide for his wants, because he was a prophet of the Lord.

When old and unable to work, he frequently came to my house, and would follow my wife about the house and talk Mormonism to her several days at a time.

When she could endure it no longer, she longer she would ask him if the Lord told him to marry Caroline Young, his second wife, who left him and went to Utah. He always became angry at that and would leave.

—Stephen H. Hart, *Naked Truths about Mormonism* 1, no. 2 (April 1888):3.

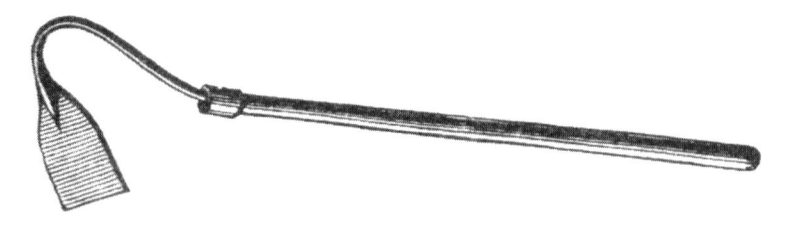

Samuel Whitney

SAMUEL F. WHITNEY was Newel K. Whitney's brother. After the departure of the Saints, Samuel remained in the Kirtland area.

ALL THE TIME Martin was in Kirtland boys eight years and older would gather about him and dispute with, and annoy him in various ways. Martin claimed to be Elijah and when greatly annoyed would curse them. The boys would say, "Go up old bald head, now fetch on your bears."

The last years of his stay in Kirtland he suffered extreme poverty and would have been much better off in the poor-house. I told my nephew, Bishop Orson F. Whitney, from Salt Lake City, when he visited me and other leading Mormons, it was a disgrace for them to permit Martin who was one of the three witnesses and had spent his estate in promulgating Mormonism, to suffer as he did. Soon after they took him to Utah, where he lived a few years and died, aged ninety-three.

—"Statement of Rev. S. F. Whitney," 6 March 1885, *Naked Truths about Mormonism* 1, no. 1 (April 1888):3.

Orson F. Whitney

William Homer, 1869

IN 1869, WILLIAM Harrison Homer was travelling back to Salt Lake City after completing his English mission. Homer's sister married Martin Harris's son, Martin Harris Jr. Homer decided to stop to see Martin Harris and tour the Kirtland Temple. On 14 December 1869, William H. Homer and his cousin, James A. Crockett, signed the Temple Visitors Ledger.

I FIRST SAW MARTIN Harris in Kirtland, Ohio, about the last of December, 1869. On my return from a mission to England, I stopped to visit some of my relatives in Pennsylvania. On resuming my journey, one of my cousins, James A. Crockett, who was not a member of the Church, came as far as Kirtland, Ohio, with me. We remained in Kirtland over night, and the next morning after breakfast we asked the landlord who was custodian of the Mormon temple at Kirtland, and he informed us that Martin Harris was custodian and pointed out to us where we would find the old gentleman. Accordingly we went to the door and knocked. In answer to our knock there came to the door of the cottage a poorly clad, emaciated little man, on whom the winter of life was weighing heavily. It was Martin Harris. In his face might be read the story of his life. There were the marks of spiritual upliftment. There were the marks of keen disappointment. There was the hunger strain for the peace, the contentment, the divine calm that it seemed could come no more into his life. It was a pathetic figure, and yet it was a figure of strength. For with it all there was something about the little man which revealed the fact that he had lived richly; that into his life had entered such noble experiences as come to the lives of but few.

I introduced myself modestly as a brother-in-law of Martin Harris, Jr. as he had married my eldest sister and as an elder of the Church who was returning from a foreign mission. The effect of the introduction was electric. But the fact of relationship was overwhelmed by the fact of Utah citizenship. The old man bristled with vindictiveness. "One of those Brighamite Mormons, are you?" he snapped. Then he railed impatiently against Utah and the founder of the Mormon commonwealth. It was in vain that I tried to turn the old man's attention to his family. Martin Harris seemed to be obsessed. He would not understand that there stood before him a man who knew his wife and children; who had followed the Church to Utah.

After some time, however, the old man said, "You want to see the temple, do you?" "Yes, indeed," I exclaimed, "if we may." "Well, I'll get the key," he answered. From that moment, Martin Harris, in spite of occasional outbursts, radiated with interest. He led us through the rooms of the temple and explained how they were used. He pointed out the place of the school of the prophets. He showed where the temple curtain had at one time hung. He related thrilling experiences in connection with the history of the sacred building. In the basement, as elsewhere, there were many signs of dilapidation: the plaster had fallen off the ceilings and the walls; windows were broken; the woodwork was stained and marred. Whether it was the influence of these conditions or not it is difficult to tell, but here again Martin Harris was moved to speak against the Utah Mormons. An injustice, a gross injustice had been done to him. He should have been chosen president of the Church.

When the old man was somewhat exhausted, I asked, "Is it not true that you were once very prominent in the Church; that you gave liberally of your means, that you were very active in the performance of your duties?" "That is very true," replied Martin. "Things were all right then. I was honored [sic] while the people were here, but now that I am old and poor it is all different."

"Really," I replied, "how can that be? What about your testimony of the Book of Mormon? Do you still believe that the Book of Mormon is true and that Joseph Smith was a prophet?" Again the effect was electric. A changed old man stood before me. It was no longer a man with an imagined grievance. It was a man with a message, a man with a noble conviction in his heart, a man inspired of God and endowed with divine knowledge. Through the broken window of the temple shone the winter sun, clear and radiant.

"Young man," answered Martin

William Harrison Homer

Harris with impressiveness, "Do I believe it! Do you see the sun shining! Just as surely as the sun is shining on us and gives us light, and the moon and stars give us light by night, just as surely as the breath of life sustains us, so surely do I know that Joseph Smith was a true prophet of God, chosen of God to open the last dispensation of the fullness of times; so surely do I know that the Book of Mormon was divinely translated. I saw the plates; I saw the angel; I heard the voice of God. I know that the Book of Mormon is true and that Joseph Smith was a true Prophet of God. I might as well doubt my own existence as to doubt the divine authenticity of the Book of Mormon, or the divine calling of Joseph Smith."

It was a sublime moment. It was a wonderful testimony. We were thrilled to the very roots of our hair.

Martin Harris, Temple Guide, by Anne Romig

The shabby, emaciated little man before us was transformed as he stood before us with hand outstretched toward the sun of heaven. A halo seemed to encircle him. A divine fire glowed in his eyes. His voice throbbed with sincerity and the conviction of his message. It was the real Martin Harris, whose burning testimony no power on earth could quench. It was the most thrilling moment of my life.

I asked Martin Harris how he could bear such a wonderful testimony after having left the Church. He said, "Young man, I never did leave the Church; the Church left me."

Martin Harris was now in a softer mood. He turned to me and asked, "Who are you?" I explained again our relationship. "So, my son Martin married your sister," repeated the old man, shaking my hand. "You know my family then?" "Yes," I replied. "Wouldn't you like to see your family again?" "I should like to see Caroline and the children," mused Martin naming over the children, "But I cannot, I am too poor." "That need not stand in the way," I answered, "President Young would be only too glad to furnish means to convey you to Utah." "Don't talk Brigham Young," warned Martin, "he would not do anything that was right." "Send him a message by me," I persisted, now deeply concerned in the project. "No," declared Harris emphatically, "yet, I should like to see my family." "Then entrust me with the message," I pleaded. Martin paused. "Well," he said slowly, "I believe I will. You call on Brigham Young. Tell him about our visit. Tell him that Martin Harris is an old, old man, living on charity, with his relatives. Tell him I should like to visit Utah, my family and children—I would be glad to accept help from the Church, but I want no personal favor. Wait! Tell him that if he sends money, he must send enough for the round trip. I should not want to remain in Utah." For twenty-five years he had nursed the old grudge against the leaders of the Church, probably because nobody had had the patience with him that I had shown.

After we had bidden Martin Harris good-bye, and had taken a few steps from the temple, my cousin placed his hands on my shoulders and said, "Wait a minute." Looking me squarely in the eyes, he said, "I can testify that the Book of Mormon is true. There is something within me that tells me that the old man told the truth. I know the Book of Mormon is true."

In due time I reached my home in the Seventh Ward in Salt Lake City. I recounted to my father the expe-

Crockett and Homer Signatures in Kirtland Temple Visitor's Register. 1869

rience with Martin Harris and we two set out immediately to report at the office of President Young. The president received us very graciously. He listened attentively to my recital of my visit with Martin Harris. President Young asked questions now and again to make clear on certain points. Then, when the story was told, he said, and it seemed to me that he beamed with pleasure, "I want to say this: I was never more gratified over any message in my life. Send for him! Yes, even if it were to take the last dollar of my own. Martin Harris spent his time and money freely when one dollar was worth more than one thousand dollars are worth now. Send for him! Yes, indeed I shall send!"

—William Harrison Homer, "The Passing of Martin Harris," *The Improvement Era* 29 (March 1926):468-72.

Edward Stevenson, February 1870

IN FEBRUARY 1870, Edward Stevenson, stopped to see the Kirtland Temple while on an LDS Church mission. Edward wrote:

WHILE THERE [Kirtland], I again met Martin Harris, soon after coming out of the Temple. He took from under his arm a copy of the Book of Mormon, the first edition, I believe, and bore a faithful testimony. . . . He said that it was his duty to continue to lift up his voice as he had been commanded to do in defence [defense] of the Book that he held in his hand, and offered to prove from the Bible that just such a book was to come forth out of the ground, and that, too, in a day when there were no prophets on the earth, and that he was daily bearing testimony to many who visited the Temple.

—Edward Stevenson to Editor, *Deseret News*, 30 November 1881, *Deseret Evening News* 15 (13 December 1881).

Edward Stevenson, August 1870

STEVENSON RETURNED to Utah to gather funds to move Martin west. In August, Stevenson returned for Harris. Stevenson preached twice in the Kirtland Temple and signed the visitors register:

August 7 1870
Elder Edward Stevenson visited the Temple Feb 11-1870 & alsoe [sic] on the 7th of Aug 1870 & Preached at 11 O clock & at 5 P.M. Sunday The docktrines [sic] of Joseph Smith as Revealed to him By the Angle [sic] Now Continued by Brigham Young the True Successor of Joseph the Prophet.
[inserted afterward by RLDS Guides] Emphatically Denied by the Elders of the Reorganized Church of J C of LDS.
[inserted by Stevenson on a still later visit] not my last writing Oct 2 1888, "To the Law & the testimony."

—Kirtland Temple Visitor Register, 1866-83, 51, CofChrist Archives.

Stevenson later documented his role in moving Harris to Utah:

Salt Lake City,
November 30, 1881

Editor Deseret News:

HAVING BEEN interrogated recently regarding Martin Harris... I feel prompted to offer a few facts relating to his removal from Ohio to Utah, his various testimonies, and incidents of personal observation of his life for the past 48 years....

While I was living in Michigan, then a territory, in 1833, near the town of Pontiac, Oakland County, Martin Harris came there, and in a meeting, where I was present, bore testimony of the appearance of an angel exhibiting the golden plates, and commanding him to bear a testimony of these things to all people whenever opportunity was afforded him to do so; and I can say that his testimony had great effect in that vicinity. Martin had a sister living in our neighborhood [sic] [Mrs. Naomi Bent]....

In the year 1869 I was appointed on a mission to the [eastern] United States. Having visited several of the eastern states, I called at Kirtland, Ohio, to see the first temple that was built by our people in this generation. While there, I again

MARTIN HARRIS'S KIRTLAND

Journey *to* Utah

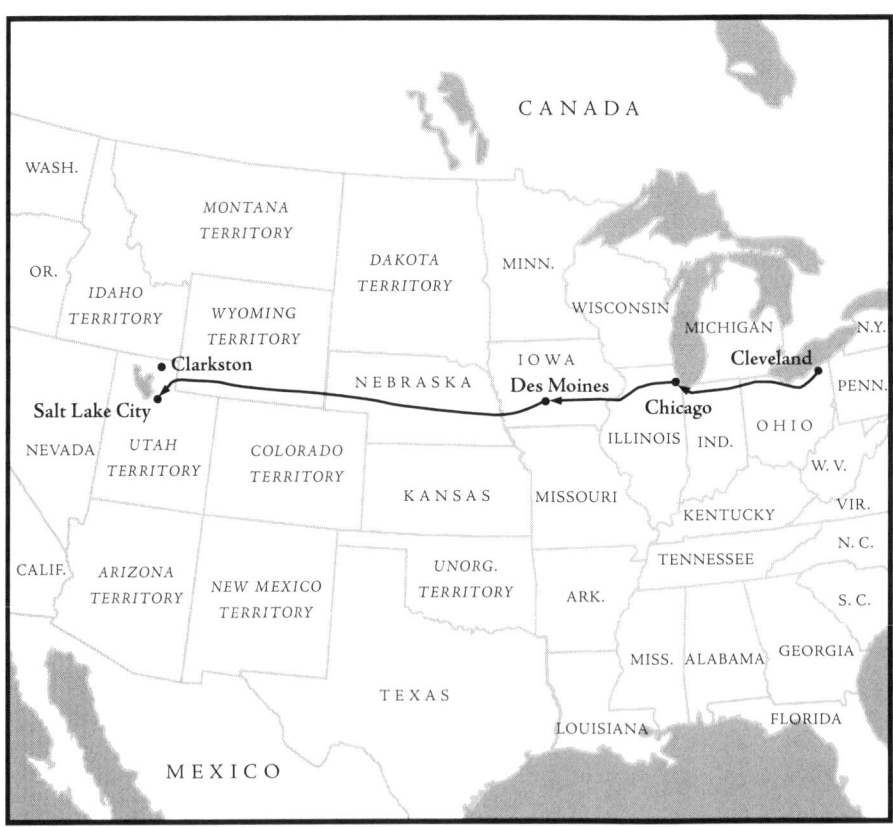

Martin Harris's Trip to Utah Territory. Map courtesy of John Hamer.

met Martin Harris, soon after coming out of the temple. He took from under his arm a copy of the Book of Mormon, the first edition, I believe, and bore a faithful testimony, just the same as that I had heard him bear 36 years previous. He said that it was his duty to continue to lift up his voice as he had been commanded to do in defense [sic] of the book that he held in his hand, and offered to prove from the Bible that just such a book was to come forth out of the ground, and that, too, in a day when there were no prophets on the earth, and that he was daily bearing testimony to many who visited the temple.

After patiently hearing him, I felt a degree of compassion for him, and in turn bore my testimony to him, as I had received it through obedience to the gospel, and that the work was still [going] onward, and the words of Isaiah, second chapter, were being fulfilled, that "the house of the Lord was in the tops of the mountains," and that under the leadership of President Brigham Young all nations were gathering to Zion to learn of God's ways and to walk in His paths, and that the worst wish that we had, was for him to also prepare himself and go up and be a partaker of the blessings of the House of the Lord. My testimony impressed him. A Mr. Bond, who held the keys of the temple, and who had been present at the dedication, and [was] then a faithful Latter-day Saint, said to me he felt as though he would have been far better off if he had kept with the Latter-day Saints, and that if I would preach in the temple, he would open the doors to me. I promised to do so at some future time.

After my arrival in Utah in 1870, I was inspired to write to Martin Harris, and soon received a reply that the Spirit of God, for the first time prompted him to go to Utah. Several letters were afterward exchanged. President Brigham Young, having read the letter, through President George A. Smith, requested me to get a subscription and emi-

Edward Stevenson

grate Martin to Utah, he subscribing twenty-five dollars for that purpose. Having raised the subscription to about $200.00, on the 19th of July, I took the railroad cars for Ohio, and on the 10th of August, filled my appointment, preaching twice in the Kirtland Temple, finding Martin Harris elated with his prospective journey....

Although in his 88th year he possessed remarkable vigor [sic] and health, having recently worked in the garden, and dug potatoes by the day for some of his neighbors [sic]....

On the 21st of August [1870], Martin was with me in Chicago, and at the American Hotel bore testimony to a large number of people, of the visitation of the angel, etc.... While in Des Moines, the capitol of Iowa, Brother Harris had opportunity of bearing testimony to many... at a special meeting held in a branch of our Church.... On the 29th of August [1870] we landed in Ogden....

Soon after receiving his blessings in the house of the Lord, he went to Smithfield, Cache Valley, and lived with his son....

—Edward Stevenson to Editor of the *Deseret News*, "One of the Three Witnesses," *Deseret News* 30, no. 40 (28 December 1881):10.

Martin's Absence

MARTIN HARRIS, while not always a practicing Latter-day Saint between 1838 and 1870, was nevertheless a powerful representation of the LDS story within the community. Harris was a tangible link between the early church experience and the second generation. Harris was a living reminder of the exhilaration of the early church experience and the spirit of the movement. While he lived at Kirtland, Martin was the Temple guide. Through his instrumentality, hundreds of visitors vicariously experienced the movement's past. Harris ended his tours with his testimony to the truth of the Book of Mormon and the Restoration work. Martin's testimony had an electrifying effect upon visitors.

The Temple remained the center of Harris's religious life. Martin was drawn to the Temple, knowing he would encounter believers. In a remarkable way Harris's very presence in Kirtland helped preserve the Temple. Just being there kept the vision of the movement alive. No doubt, the Temple also helped preserve Martin. Regular encounters with old and new friends at the Temple gave him a purpose for living. And no doubt, the influx of appreciative visitors helped supplement his meagre living.

Ironically Martin's removal to Utah signalled the end of an era and symbolically marked the end of a significant LDS presence in Kirtland. In the end, the LDS Church got Martin, the old witness, but his departure surely opened the door for others to control the structure. With Martin's absence, fewer Latter-day Saints seemed to visit Kirtland. Joseph Smith III's followers filled the void created by Harris's absence and soon controlled the House of the Lord.

ONE MORMON IN UTAH, known as "S.," recognized the value of Martin's presence at Kirtland. S. expressed this awareness in a letter addressed to the *Willoughby Independent*. S. wrote:

I SENT YOU A PAPER sometime since containing a notice of the death of the veteran Patriarch, Martin Harris, one of the three witnesses to the Book of Mormon; and may our last days be like his, full in the faith. You well know what he did for the Church in Kirtland—and is that all to be lost? We hope and believe not; for it is now under consideration among the Counselors, to send a missionary to Kirtland the coming year to rebuild Zion again....

—Reprinted in *Herald* 22, no. 22 (15 November 1875):677-78.

Martin Harris Letter, 1870

SISTER H. B. EMERSON, of New Richmond, Ohio, wrote to Martin Harris, asking specific questions. The *Herald* published Harris's reply. Harris supposed his questioner to be a man.

Smithfield, Utah,
Nov. 23d, 1870.

Mr. Emerson, Sir:—

I RECEIVED YOUR favor. In reply I will say concerning the plates, I do say that the angel did show to me the plates containing the Book of Mormon. Further, the translation that I carried to Prof. Anthon was copied from these same plates; also, that the Professor did testify to it being a correct translation. I do firmly believe and do know that Joseph Smith was a prophet of God; for without [divine aid] I know he could not had that gift; neither could he have translated the same. I can give if you require it one hundred witnesses to the proof of the Book of Mormon. I defy any man to show to me any passage of scripture that I am not posted on or familiar with. I will answer any questions you feel like asking to the best of my knowledge, if you can rely on my testimony of the same. In connection, I can say that I arrived at Utah safe, in good health and spirits, considering the long journey. I am quite well at present, and have been, generally speaking, since I arrived.

With many respects I remain your humble friend,
MARTIN HARRIS.

—Martin Harris to H. Emerson, January 1871, *Herald* 22, no. 20 (15 October 1875):630.

Martin Harris, courtesy LDS Church Archives.

Simon Smith, 1875

A letter from Simon Smith to Joseph Smith III:

> Clifton, Bristol, England
> December 29, 1880

President Joseph Smith:

YOUR FAVOR, AND Elder Mark H. Forscutt's 23rd Oct. last received. It laid some time in the P.O. here as I was away visiting some of my relatives and old friends in Wilts. I at once corresponded with Elder Thomas Taylor, and he sent me the Saints Herald for Dec. 1st inst. which contains my address to those in Utah and elsewhere adhering to and practising the doctrine of Polygamy, which according to the word of God is a corrupt doctrine. That a very noted person called "the Lion of the Lord," John Taylor The Champion of right, and Orson Pratt, "The Gauge of Philosophy" with many others, have labored very zealously for many years past trying to convert this corrupt doctrine into a pure one. Is it not astonishing that men who once lived in the light of truth should now be found using every means to establish a falsehood? In the notice of Presidents Joseph and Hyrum Smith, (*Times and Seasons* [Vol. 5], page 425), against Polygamy, and other false and corrupt doctrines, I find by comparing the address with said notice, that that part of the address which reads H. P. Brown, should read Hiram Brown. The error was made when I wrote the copy. I have often thought of writing a few lines to you (since my conversion to the doctrines of Christ for which your father spent his days and life to establish), respecting an interview I had with Martin Harris Sen. a few days before his decease.

On the 5th day of July, 1875, hearing of his sickness, I visited him, <and> as I entered the room where he was in bed he held out his hand, shook hands with me saying, "I am going to leave you now, Bishop," meaning he was going to die. At the time he was very low; and apparently, it was hard work for him to talk, but he was perfectly rational. I laid my hand on his head, and asked the Lord to give him strength. As soon as I commenced to talk to him and ask him questions respecting the Book of Mormon and your Father, he revived and talked to me very freely and with much earnestness (for about two hours).

I will give you the answers he gave me to a few prominent questions respecting his knowledge of your Father, the plates, & etc. 1st I asked him if he could still testify of seeing the plates and the angel of God. His answer was he could. And he did truly testify to me that he both saw and handled the plates that the Book of Mormon was translated from and that an angel of God did lay them before him and the other two witnesses as recorded in the Book of Mormon, and said he, I tell you of these things that you might tell others that what I have said is true, and I dare not deny it for what he had seen and had handled he had heard the voice of God commanding him to testify to the same.

He said also he knew not the reason why the Lord had suffered him to live to such a great age unless it was to testify of these things. (He was nearly 93 years old). He said also that he acted as scribe for your father when he was translating from the plates by the Urim and Thummim nearly one-third of what is published and mortgaged his property, to get the first Edition of the Book of Mormon published to the world and that he by command, took part of the manuscript with the translation to one Professor Anthony [sic], Prof. of Language, in New York City, to get his opinion in regard to the language and translation, and <that> what had been published

Charles Anthon

concerning the same was also true. And in regard to a question I asked him of your father's education at the time of those circumstances and he said Joseph Smith's education was so limited that he could not draw up a note of hand.

These were Martin Harris' exact words to me. I do not mention this part to throw any gloom upon your father's mission but to the contrary. I mention it to show it was out of his power with such a limited education to produce such a book as the Book of Mormon much less to translate such a book from [a] foreign language unless he did it by the gift and power of God. I might mention more he told me; but it is so irksome for me to write and <will> give you too much trouble to prepare it for the press, if you thought it proper to publish it. One more item however I will mention. He (Martin Harris, Sen.) assured me that polygamy was not taught or practiced by Joseph Smith nor was it a doctrine of the Church in his day.

Before the mortal remains of Martin Harris, Sen. were conveyed to its last resting place (Clarkston grave yard) I placed in his right hand a Book of Mormon, which was buried with the remains. Some might think that a strange affair but I did it out of respect for a man so highly favored of the Lord and the interest he took to help to bring forth to the world a record of divine truth. I had a head board placed at his grave, on it written his name, nativity, and age; also his testimony concerning the plates & etc., as recorded in the forepart of the Book of Mormon. Your Bro. in the cause of truth, Simon Smith.

—Simon Smith to Mark H. Forscutt, 29 December 1880, holograph Miscellaneous Letters and Papers, P13, f268, CofChrist Archives; printed in *Saints' Herald* 28 (1 February 1881):43.

Death *of* Martin Harris

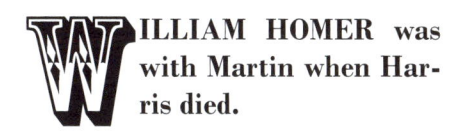

WILLIAM HOMER was with Martin when Harris died.

. . . Early in July, 1875, five years after he had come to Utah, Martin Harris was stricken with a kind of paralysis. It was the venerable witness' last illness, but through it all he remained true to his faith. At that time I and my small family lived in Clarkston. With other members of the Clarkston ward, I called at the Harris home to relieve them in the care of the old man.

We began to think that he had borne his last testimony. The last audible words he had spoken were something about the Book of Mormon but we could not understand what it was, but these were not the aged witness' last words.

The next day, July 10, 1875, marked the end. It was in the evening. It was milking time, and Martin Harris, Jr., and his wife, Nancy Homer Harris, had gone out to milk and to do the evening's chores. In the house with the stricken man were left my mother, Eliza Williamson Homer, and myself, who had had so interesting a day with Martin Harris in Kirtland.

I stood by the bedside, holding the patient's right hand and my mother at the foot of the bed. Martin Harris had been unconscious for a number of days. When we first entered the room the old gentleman appeared to be sleeping. He soon woke up and asked for a drink of water. I put my arm under the old gentleman, raised him, and my mother held the glass to his lips. He drank freely, then he looked up at me and recognized me. He said, "I know you. You are my friend." He said, "Yes, I did see the plates on which the Book of Mormon was written; I did see the angel; I did hear the voice of God; and I do know that Joseph Smith is a Prophet of God, holding the keys of the holy priesthood." This was the end. Martin Harris, divinely-chosen witness of the work of God, relaxed, gave up my hand. He lay back on his pillow and just as the sun went down behind the Clarkston mountains, the soul of Martin Harris passed on. When Martin Harris, Jr., and his wife returned to the house they found that their father had passed away, but in the passing, Martin Harris, favored of God, repeated an irrefutable testimony of the divine inspiration and the prophetic genius of the great Prophet, Joseph Smith. (Signed) William Harrison Homer.

—William Harrison Homer, Sr., "The Passing of Martin Harris," *The Improvement Era* 29 (March 1926):468-72.

Martin Harris Obituary

ON JULY 10, 1875, Martin Harris died at Clarkston, Cache County, Utah. The following obituary was prepared by his son and published in the Ogden Junction:

Died at Clarkston, Cache County, Utah, July 10, 1875, of old age, Martin Harris, Sr.; aged 92 years, 1 month, and 22 days.

Deceased was born May 18, 1783, at Easttown, Saratoga County, in the state of New York, from which place he moved with his father's family in his ninth year to the town of Palmyra, Ontario County (now Wayne), in the same State. In the fall of 1827 he became acquainted with the Prophet Joseph Smith, and learned all the facts about the Book of Mormon, and became perfectly satisfied in his own mind of its divine origin. Without delay or hesitation he identified himself with the Prophet Joseph Smith, and from that time forward rendered him every assistance in his power to forward the divine work, and to establish the true church of Christ upon the earth in this dispensation.

He went, by the request of the Prophet Joseph Smith, to the city of New York and presented a transcript of the records of the Book of Mormon to Professor Anthon and Doctor Mitchill [sic] and asked them to translate it. He also presented the same transcript to many other learned men at the different schools of learning in Geneva, Utica, and Albany with the same request, but was unsuccessful in obtaining the translation of the transcript from any of them. After his return from the city of New York he was employed as scribe to the Prophet Joseph in the translation of the records of the Book of Mormon.

After the translation was completed he was called by divine revelation to be one of the three witnesses of the Book of Mormon. The testimony of the three witnesses forms part of the preface to the book. He paid for the printing of five thousand copies and labored as proof-reader of the book. He traveled some two thousand five hundred miles in its interest before the book was printed, and bore his own expenses.

He was one of the six members at the organization of the church on April 6, 1830. He was one of the members of the first High Council. He attended the first public meeting, at which Oliver Cowdery preached the first public discourse on the principles of the gospel as revealed through the Prophet Joseph Smith in this dispensation. He attended the first conference of the church held at Fayette, Seneca County, state of New York.

He moved with the church to Kirtland, Ohio, where the first temple was built. He went up to Missouri in company with the Prophet Joseph Smith and others, at the time when they were afflicted with the cholera, and was one of those who were afflicted, but was healed instantly by the power of God. He was one who witnessed the dispersing of the mob by a terrible storm, which, while it proved fatal to many of the mob, brought salvation to the Saints. He was one who assisted in purchasing land in Missouri for the gathering of the Saints, he having paid Bishop Partridge the sum of one thousand two hundred dollars.

He was present at the dedication of the Kirtland Temple, and witnessed the powerful manifestations of God on that memorable occasion. He figured conspicuously in nearly all of the early movements of the church, and was one who never withheld his substance or means when it was required to establish and forward the interests of the church. He always thought and said that his mission was to stay in Kirtland, where the first temple was built, so he did not move with the church, but remained in Kirtland till the year 1870, when he came to Utah.

Since coming to Utah he has resided with his son, Martin Harris, Jr., in Cache County. He was in his eighty-eighth year when he came to this Territory. He has enjoyed good health and a good appetite, and has been industrious; all the time since his arrival. He would never be idle so long as there was anything that he could do. He has always borne a faithful and undeviating testimony to the divinity of the Book of Mormon, whether in Kirtland, in the midst of the wicked and ungodly, or in Utah, or any of the different places where the Saints have resided. He was in his happiest mood when he could get somebody to listen to his testimony, and he never appeared to get tired of talking about the coming forth of the Book of Mormon, and testifying to its truth. And if at any time he felt dull or tired from any cause whatever, and he could get an opportunity of testifying to the truth of that book, he would revive immediately.

His health first began to fail him about eight or nine days previous to his death. He first experienced severe pains in his legs, and finally lost the use of his limbs, so that he became entirely helpless, and was confined to his bed. He continued to talk at intervals until a few hours before his death. His last audible words were something about the Book of Mormon and the three witnesses. He sank gradually day after day, and finally expired on Saturday, July 10, 1875.

MARTIN HARRIS, JR.

—Reprinted in *Saints' Herald* 22, no. 17 (1 September 1875):541-42.

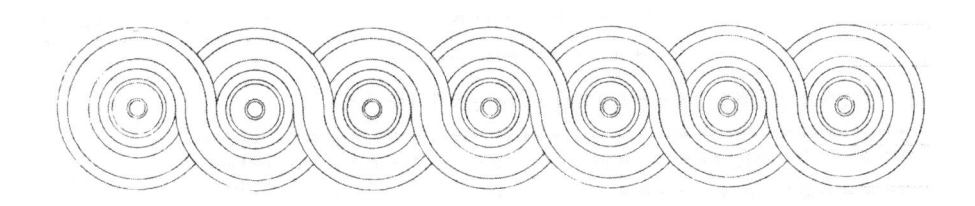

Martin's Funeral

Harris's son writes:

WE HAD A GOOD attendance and a large turn out for a small town like Clarkston. Every respect that could be paid to him was manifested by the people. We put the Book of Mormon in his right hand, and the Book of Covenants in his left hand. We had a very good coffin, and finished very nicely. We inscribed on the head board the following: His name, and birth, and age, and place of birth, and also his death, with the words—"'One of the three Witnesses of the book of Mormon, also their Testimony.'"

There were 16 teams or wagons, well filled with the people, who entertained a kind regard for old brother Martin.

—"Martin Harris," *Deseret News* 24, no. 26 (28 July 1875):2.

Martin Harris Monument, Clarkston, Utah

Interview *with* Marin Harris *in* Rhyme

A poem by William Pilkington.

IN OCTOBER OF THE fall of seventy-four,
I met an aged man who I had never seen before
His steps were feeble, but his eyes were bright
And in them gleamed, intelligence and light.

He was a living witness with eleven
of Ministrations from the courts of Heaven,
Nine of those witnesses have passed away.
And he had then, little time to stay....

"Pray, is it true," I asked that you have been
With heavenly messengers and have seen,
The records called the plates of brass and gold,
Of which Moroni, in his Book has told?

"Tis said you saw an angel from on high,
While other witnesses were standing by,
And that the messengers commanded you,
To testify that this strange work is true.

Not questioning your statement that I've read,
Or what the other witness' have said,
But I would like to know from you direct,
If we have read or heard those things correct?

He lifted up his voice and thus replied
My written statement I have ne'er denied,
I saw the angel, and I heard his voice,
And wondrous things that made my heart rejoice.

This interview was sought with earnest prayer,
The Prophet, and three witnesses were there.
But Martin, conscious-stricken, declined to stay.
And wandered off alone to watch and pray.

I do not know the angel's rank or name,
Who on this great and glorious mission came,
I know that he was clothed in power and might
And was surrounded with effulgent light.

No tongue can tell the glory and the power
That was revealed to us in that blessed hour,
The plates of brass and gold the angel took
and placed before us like an open book.

What Martin Harris said, the people know
May be regarded as precisely so.
He's not a man to shade the truth, or lie.
For on his word you can, for sure, rely.

—By William Pilkington, Smithfield, Utah, cited in Vogel, ***Early Mormon Documents*** 2:363-64.

Additional Reading *about* Martin Harris:

Richard L. Anderson, *Investigating the Book of Mormon Witnesses* (Salt Lake City, Utah: Deseret Book Company, 1981).

Wayne Cutler Gunnell, "Martin Harris-Witness and Benefactor to the Book of Mormon," M.A. thesis, Department of Religion, Brigham Young University, June 1955.

Madge Harris Tuckett and Belle Harris Wilson, *The Martin Harris Story: With Biographies of Emer Harris and Dennison Lot Harris* (Provo, Utah: Vintage Books, 1983).

Rhett Stephens James, "Harris, Martin," *Encyclopedia of Mormonism*, 4 Vols (New York: Macmillan Publishing, 1992), 2: 574-76.

Christin Craft Mackay and Lachlan Mackay, "A Time of Transition: The Kirtland Temple, 1838-1800," *John Whitmer Historical Association Journal* 18 (1998):133-48.

H. Michael Marquardt, "Martin Harris: The Kirtland Years, 1831-1870," *Dialogue: A Journal of Mormon Thought*, 35, no. 3 (Fall 2002):1-40.

Eldin Ricks, *The Case of the Book of Mormon Witnesses*, Salt Lake City, Utah: Deseret News Press, 1971.

Dan Vogel, ed., *Early Mormon Documents* Vol. 2 (Salt Lake City, Utah: Signature Books, 1998).

Walker, Ronald W. "Martin Harris: Mormonism's Early Convert." *Dialogue: A Journal of Mormon Thought* 19 (Winter 1986): 29–43.